edexcel
advancing learning, changing lives

# Aim High

## in Edexcel GCSE English

Roger Addison

Peter Huke

Pam Taylor

Contributor: Mandy Hill

Series editor: Duncan Beal

A PEARSON COMPANY

# Contents

# Introduction

## TO THE STUDENT

This book is for anyone following the Edexcel GCSE English course. Whether you are following Specification A (English A, 1203) or Specification B (English B, 1204), Higher or Foundation Tier, you will find lots of relevant material to help you practise the skills required for success at GCSE English.

## How will this book help me?

This book teaches essential skills and techniques that will help you improve your grade for each section of the examinations in GCSE English. It is written by senior examiners who each year see hundreds of examination papers. They know the skills that candidates need to gain marks; they also know how candidates could do better. In this book they share that knowledge with you. The activities are designed to build up your understanding and confidence, then give you practice on each skill.

## How should I use this book?

You can use this book by working through the sections you are studying in order or by dipping into different sections as you want to use them. If you work through each section as it is laid out in this book, you will build up practice in the essential skills for that section of the examination. At the end of each section there are example answers that show you the skills in practice and illustrate what you need to do to achieve high grades. Finally, you have a chance to put it all together by practising with past examination questions, where appropriate.

Whether you are using this book for class study or for individual revision at home, we hope you will find it useful in improving the skills required to achieve high grades. We wish you all success.

## TO THE TEACHER

### How is *Aim High in Edexcel GCSE English* organised?

This book takes you through each section of the two GCSE English papers, so you can be confident that your students have tackled the skills that have been identified as making a key diffference to results for each paper. The sections you are teaching vary depending on whether you choose to take Specification A (English A, 1203) or Specification B (English B, 1204).

In either case, each examination comprises three sections, and each section requires the student to answer one question. Each question is worth 10% of their total mark in GCSE English.

The sections in this book relate directly to the sections in the examination papers (see the chart on page 5).

### Assessment objectives/mark scheme

Pages 6–9 outline the assessment objectives for reading and writing, and 'unpack' them in two ways:

❖ They are broken down into their constituent parts and described in student-friendly language (pages 6 and 8).

❖ They are 'translated' into two charts showing how the students can improve their skills across the different criteria for assessing reading and writing (pages 7 and 9). These 'Steps to success' charts are simplified versions of the mark schemes used by examiners.

❖ The 'In The Exam' box at the beginning of each section notes which assessment objectives will be assessed in that section of the exam.

# How to use this book

This chart shows what the Edexcel GCSE English examination contains, and where you can revise and practise the skills in this book.

First of all, make sure you know whether you are taking Specification A (GCSE English A, 1203) or Specification B (GCSE English B, 1204). Specification A is covered on the top half of the chart. Specification B is covered on the lower half of the chart.

You should also check which collection of poetry you are studying in Section A.

**SPECIFICATION A (English A, 1203)**

| Examination topic | Skills practised in this book |
| --- | --- |
| Examination One (2 hours) <br> *The Craft of the Writer* | Foundation Tier = Paper 2F <br> Higher Tier = Paper 4H |
| ❖ Modern Poetry (Anthology) ⟶ | Section A Reading modern poetry (pages 10–44) |
| ❖ Non-fiction (Anthology) ⟶ | Section B Reading non-fiction prose (pages 45–61) |
| ❖ Writing to inform/explain/describe ⟶ | Section D Writing to inform, explain, describe (pages 79–91) |
| Examination Two (2 hours) | Foundation Tier = Paper 3F <br> Higher Tier = Paper 5H |
| ❖ Media texts (Unseen) ⟶ | Section E Reading media (pages 92–110) |
| ❖ Writing to argue/persuade/advise ⟶ | Section G Writing to argue, persuade, advise (pages 129–142) |
| ❖ Writing to analyse/review/comment ⟶ | Section H Writing to analyse, review, comment (pages 143–157) |

**SPECIFICATION B (English B, 1204)**

| Examination topic | Skills practised in this book |
| --- | --- |
| Examination One (2 hours) <br> *The Craft of the Writer* | Foundation Tier = Paper 2F <br> Higher Tier = Paper 4H |
| ❖ Modern Poetry (Anthology) ⟶ | Section A Reading modern poetry (pages 10–44) |
| ❖ Different Cultures (Anthology) ⟶ | Section C Reading short stories from different cultures and traditions (pages 62–78) |
| ❖ Writing to inform/explain/describe ⟶ | Section D Writing to inform, explain, describe (pages 79–91) |
| Examination Two (2 hours) | Foundation Tier = Paper 3F <br> Higher Tier = Paper 5H |
| ❖ Non-fiction (Unseen) ⟶ | Section F Reading non-fiction texts (unseen) (pages 111–128) |
| ❖ Writing to argue/persuade/advise ⟶ | Section G Writing to argue, persuade, advise (pages 129–142) |
| ❖ Writing to analyse/review/comment ⟶ | Section H Writing to analyse, review, comment (pages 143–157) |

# The reading skills that you will be assessed on

Three of the six questions in your GCSE English exam will be reading tasks. In Examination One, you will have studied the texts in class. In Examination Two, you will not have seen the texts before.

In the reading tasks, no marks are awarded for the accuracy of your spelling, punctuation or grammar. Instead, the examiners look at your understanding of the texts. Examiners use 'assessment objectives' to give you a mark for your work. These are outlined in the left-hand column of the table below. The right-hand column explains in more detail what you have to do to get good marks.

| Assessment objective | | To get good marks … |
|---|---|---|
| Read with insight and engagement | AO2(i) | You need to understand the texts well and show the depth of your understanding in your answer. |
| Make appropriate references to texts | | You need to support your ideas by referring to the texts, often in the form of short quotations. |
| Develop and sustain interpretations of texts | | You need to develop your answer from an effective opening through a series of paragraphs to a satisfying conclusion. Your interpretation can include a personal response to the texts. |
| Distinguish between fact and opinion | AO2(ii)* | You need to show your understanding of how media texts use facts and statistics in reporting or in support of views, and your understanding of how these differ from expressions of opinion. |
| Evaluate how information is presented | | You need to comment on the effectiveness of a media text, for example whether a news story is clearly reported, or whether an advertisement is persuasive. |
| Follow an argument, identifying implications and recognising inconsistencies | AO2(iii)* | You need to show understanding of a writer's line of argument in a media text, for example the development of ideas in a newspaper editorial. This includes recognising if an argument is not logical, or if persuasive techniques are emotive or dishonest. |
| Select material appropriate to their purpose, collate material from different sources, and make cross references | AO2(iv)* | You need to be able to see similarities and differences between texts, and to refer to examples from different texts to back up your points. |
| Understand and evaluate how writers use linguistic devices | | You need to show your understanding of writers' techniques such as choice of words, and the use of devices such as similes and alliteration. You also need to evaluate (comment on the effectiveness of) these devices. |
| Understand and evaluate how writers use structural and presentational devices | AO2(v) | You need to show that you are aware of how writers organise their texts: how they start and finish; the order of paragraphs; how they vary their sentence structure. In a media text, this includes headlines, font, colour and other aspects of visual layout. |
| Comment on ways language varies and changes | | You need to show that you understand how writers use language differently for different purposes and audiences. |

\* Note: Assessment objectives 2(ii) and 2(iii) are tested only in the Media reading task (Specification A, papers 3F or 5H). Assessment objectives 2(i), 2(iv) and 2(v) are tested in all of the reading tasks.

# Steps to success in reading

The grid on page 6 shows you in general what you have to do to meet the assessment objectives. The ladder below shows you in more detail how the examiners mark your work.

The left-hand column shows the mark band. The other columns outline what your essay must achieve in the different categories to gain a mark in that mark band. To aim for a C you need to make sure your performance is consistently at the upper end of Band 3, and for an A* you need to go for Band 5.

You can use this ladder to assess in detail how good your practice answers are. If you find you need to improve in one of the categories, that's the one to focus on in your revision and practice.

| Mark band | Understanding and interpretation of text | Understanding and evaluation of writer's use of language* | Selection and development of material/textual references |
|---|---|---|---|
| 5 | ❖ impressive command and cogent interpretation of the text | ❖ penetrating analysis and sophisticated evaluation of the writer's use of language | ❖ a variety of astute and discriminating points<br>❖ commanding exploration of ideas<br>❖ deft use of apposite examples/references |
| 4 | ❖ a thorough or assured understanding of the text<br>❖ a thoughtful or perceptive interpretation | ❖ a good or confident analysis of language<br>❖ a thoughtful or sensitive evaluation of language | ❖ a variety of well-focused or perceptive points<br>❖ ideas sustained or fully developed<br>❖ apt use of examples/references, or effective use of apposite examples/references |
| 3 | ❖ sound grasp of the text<br>❖ a secure interpretation of the text | ❖ a fair or clear understanding of language<br>❖ a sound evaluation of language | ❖ mostly clear points, or a range of relevant points<br>❖ reasonable development of ideas<br>❖ appropriate examples/references |
| 2 | ❖ some, or a fair, understanding of the text<br>❖ some interpretation of the text | ❖ limited, or some, understanding of language<br>❖ little or no attempt to evaluate language | ❖ some relevant points, or valid points<br>❖ limited or some development of ideas<br>❖ little or some relevant textual support |
| 1 | ❖ rudimentary or basic understanding of the text<br>❖ no interpretation of the text | ❖ minimal or little awareness of language<br>❖ no attempt to evaluate language | ❖ extremely limited content, or unclear and/or undeveloped points |

*NB 'Use of language' can include structural and presentational devices, although this is only required by specific questions.*

# The writing skills that you will be assessed on

Three of the six questions in your GCSE English exam will be writing tasks. Each question focuses on a different type of writing (for example, to inform or to argue).

In the writing tasks, all the marks are awarded for the quality of your writing. The examiners check how well you express your ideas, your choice of words, and the accuracy of your spelling, punctuation and grammar. Examiners use 'assessment objectives' to give you a mark for your work. These are outlined in the left-hand column of the table below. The right-hand column explains in more detail what you have to do to get good marks.

| Assessment objective | | To get good marks … |
|---|---|---|
| Communicate clearly and imaginatively | AO3(i) | You need to write lively, interesting answers which will engage the reader. You have to express yourself clearly, and use words in a way that suits the task. |
| Use and adapt different forms of writing for different readers and purposes | | You need to be able to write in different forms (e.g. a letter, a speech or an article) for a variety of audiences (e.g. classmates or adults). This means you need to have the audience and purpose of the task clearly in mind. |
| Organise ideas into sentences, paragraphs and whole texts | AO3(ii) | You need to show that you can write an arresting opening, then a clear sequence of paragraphs, and build up to a convincing conclusion. The piece must 'hang together' well. |
| Use a variety of linguistic features | | You need to use appropriate techniques such as employing powerful adjectives, adverbs, nouns and verbs; imagery (similes, metaphors); repetition; contrast; lists and direct appeals to the reader. |
| Use a variety of structural features | | You need to use appropriate techniques such as subheadings or bullet points in a report, or headlines in an article, or referring back to your opening in your conclusion. |
| Use a range of sentence structures effectively | AO3(iii) | You need to show your understanding of how sentences of different lengths and types (e.g. questions, commands, complex sentences) can be used for different effects. |
| Use accurate punctuation and spelling | | You need to show that you can use the full range of punctuation confidently and correctly, use a wide vocabulary and spell accurately. |

Note: All of these assessment objectives are tested in all of the three writing tasks.

The grid above shows you in general what you have to do to meet the assessment objectives. The ladder on page 9 shows you in more detail how the examiners mark your work.

The left-hand column shows the mark band. The other columns outline what your writing must achieve in the different categories to gain a mark in that mark band. To aim for a C you need to make sure your performance is consistently at the upper end of Band 3, and for an A* you need to go for Band 5.

You can use this ladder to assess in detail how good your practice answers are. If you find you need to improve in one of the categories, that's the one to focus on in your revision.

# Steps to success in writing

| Mark band | Purpose and audience | Effectiveness of communication | Organisation | Punctuation, grammar and spelling |
|---|---|---|---|---|
| 5 | ❖ strong fulfilment of purpose of writing<br>❖ sharply focused on audience<br>❖ addresses the writing form with precision and clarity | ❖ compelling communication<br>❖ extensive vocabulary<br>❖ mature control of sentence structure | ❖ assured organisation<br>❖ sophisticated control of text structure<br>❖ skilfully sustained paragraphing<br>❖ effective cohesive devices* | ❖ precise control of full range of punctuation<br>❖ ambitious and assured grammatical structuring<br>❖ extremely accurate spelling of wide vocabulary |
| 4 | ❖ secure realisation of purpose of writing<br>❖ secure realisation of audience<br>❖ effectively addresses the writing form | ❖ effective communication<br>❖ aptly chosen vocabulary<br>❖ well-controlled variety of sentence structure | ❖ secure organisation<br>❖ well-judged text structure<br>❖ effective paragraphing<br>❖ good use of cohesive devices* | ❖ wide range of accurate punctuation<br>❖ appropriate grammatical structures used effectively<br>❖ spelling of good range of vocabulary mostly accurate |
| 3 | ❖ clear sense of purpose of writing<br>❖ clear awareness of audience<br>❖ secure grasp of the writing form | ❖ clear communication<br>❖ well-chosen vocabulary<br>❖ evidence of crafting in sentence structure | ❖ sound organisation<br>❖ clear text structure<br>❖ controlled paragraphing<br>❖ sound use of cohesive devices* | ❖ control of punctuation mostly secure<br>❖ grammar mostly accurate<br>❖ accurate spelling of wide range of words |
| 2 | ❖ some grasp of purpose of writing and audience<br>❖ some awareness of the writing form | ❖ appropriate communication<br>❖ some control of vocabulary<br>❖ reasonable control of sentence structure | ❖ some grasp of text structure, including opening and development<br>❖ appropriate paragraphing<br>❖ limited use of cohesive devices* | ❖ basic punctuation mostly correct<br>❖ basic grammar usually correct<br>❖ spelling of common words usually accurate |
| 1 | ❖ little awareness of purpose of writing<br>❖ little sense of audience<br>❖ limited evidence of the writing form | ❖ basic communication<br>❖ limited vocabulary<br>❖ lack of variety of sentence structure | ❖ simple organisation<br>❖ limited success in opening/development<br>❖ very little use of cohesive devices* | ❖ some control of basic punctuation<br>❖ some control of grammar<br>❖ spelling of common words often correct |

*cohesive devices = ways of making the text hang together well, e.g. repetition of words/structures, use of synonyms/contrasts

# A Reading modern poetry

- There are two questions on the collection of poems you are studying. You only need to answer one.
- The question is worth 10% of your total mark for GCSE English.
- You must answer the question in 40 minutes.
- Your answer to this question will be assessed against Reading assessment objectives (i) and (v). See page 6.

By the end of this section you will have sharpened three skills that will help you to improve your answer on modern poetry:

**1** plan your answer so that you write about two poems in a balanced way

**2** write a clear opening that shows the shape your answer will take

**3** comment effectively on how the poets use language.

You will also explore answers at different grades and assess your skills through writing an answer to a poetry question that is similar to the one you will meet in the exam.

## Reading modern poetry

The poems are divided into three collections, which are:

♦ *In Such a Time as This*, which includes poems with a distinctive sense of time and place

♦ *Identity*, which focuses on how individuals develop and change through their lives

♦ *Nature*, which contains responses to the natural world.

You are studying the poems in only *one* of these collections, which are covered in different units in this section: *In Such a Time as This* (pages 11–21), *Identity* (pages 22–33), *Nature* (pages 34–44).

## What is the examiner looking for?

Below are the characteristics of a good answer and of a weak answer. Find the pairs of comments that match. This activity will focus your attention on the qualities that will gain you marks in this section of the exam. The first pair has been done for you.

| A good answer | A weak answer |
|---|---|
| • writes equally about both poems and links them well | • writes only about one poem or offers little on the second poem with no attempt to link the two |

**H** focuses on what the poems are about, rather than the poets' technique

**A** uses textual evidence to support its ideas

**C** writes equally about both poems and links them well

**D** fails to back up its points with evidence from the text

**E** writes about the story in the poems but ignores features of language and verse

**G** writes only about one poem or offers little on the second poem with no attempt to link the two

**B** shows understanding of the ways poets use language

**F** comments on features of poems such as rhyme, rhythm, sound effects, long or short lines and verses

## 1 Plan a balanced answer

Always read the question carefully and spend around 5–10 minutes planning your answer. First work out what the focus of the question is by noting the key words.

1 Read the examiner comments about the key words in the question below.

Rejection is the focus of the question, the link between the two poems. There is always a focus – the question never says 'Write all you know about these two poems'!

The question asks you to make a judgement about how well the poet conveys thoughts and feelings.

Look again at *Refugee Blues* and *You Will Be Hearing From Us Shortly*.

Both these poems involve feelings of rejection. How successfully, and by what methods, do the writers convey their thoughts and feelings?

In your answer you should make close reference to the language of the poems.

How are the points conveyed? What techniques of language or verse do the poets use?

You need to make interesting comments about how poets use language for effect, and support your comments with short quotations from the poems.

The question is not just about the content of the poems, but the poets' attitudes towards their subjects.

**EXAM TIP**

Underline key words in the question in the exam and use them to help you plan. Use them throughout the essay, and at the end check back to make sure you have covered them in your answer. Foundation Tier questions will have bullet points to guide you in your answer. Make sure you write something on each of them.

2 Now read the following question. With a partner decide which are the key words and why. Then compare your ideas with others.

Look again at *Hide and Seek* and *Brendon Gallacher*.

In what ways do the poets show the importance to children of the power of imagination?

In your answer you should make close reference to the language of the poems.

## Plan your answer

When you have highlighted your key words and got a firm grip on the question, you need to plan and shape your answer.

3 Read the student plan and examiner comments on the next page. You will use what you find out to write your own plan.

Look again at *Refugee Blues* and You *Will Be Hearing From Us Shortly*.

Both these poems involve feelings of **rejection**. How **successfully**, and by what **methods**, do the writers convey their **thoughts and feelings**?

In your answer you should make **close reference to the language** of the poems.

**1**
- ✓ gives a broad initial response to the question showing the overall view
- ✓ shows the student is addressing the focus of the question (rejection)
- ✓ sets up the shape of the essay

**2–3**
- ✓ discusses rejection
- ✓ shows some of the methods the poet uses to convey thoughts and feelings
- ✓ explores thoughts and feelings
- ✓ makes close reference to the language of the poem
- ✓ uses lots of short quotations to support points made

**4**
- ✓ makes good links of similarities and differences
- ✓ shows balanced coverage of both poems

**5**
- ✓ rounds off the answer
- ✓ sums up the main points
- ✓ refers back to the original question and key points
- ✓ gives the student's own view

1. Introduction

Yes, they're both about rejection.

Both successful, but different tones and methods.

Write about each poem in turn, talking about the themes as they occur.

2. 'Refugee Blues'

Context: political, serious, German Jews – 'It was Hitler over Europe'

Scale: large scale, about major events, 'ten thousand soldiers', 'thunder rumbling'

But focuses on individuals and their suffering – 'steal our daily bread', 'my dear'

Structure and style: Blues – reflects the 'blue' mood

Language and tone: nostalgia – 'old yew ... blossoms anew'

Feelings: rejection, powerlessness, loss –'where shall we go today?'

3. 'You Will Be Hearing From Us Shortly'

Context: interview

Scale: personal, individual – 'domestic disasters'

Structure and style: only interviewer's words given – the interviewee is nothing. Reader is addressed, as if interviewee – 'you ... you'

Language and tone: formal, sarcastic – 'might they, perhaps, find your appearance disturbing?'

Humour: sarcasm and putdowns funny to an outsider – 'So glad we agree', 'Yes. Pity'

Feelings: rejection, humiliation – 'were you educated?', 'unsuitable address'

4. Comparing the poems

Very different structure, setting and techniques

The big picture given in 'Refugee Blues', but both deal with individual rejection

Different language: harsh and formal in YW, softer and lyrical in RB – but feelings of powerlessness and rejection come across strongly in both

5. Conclusion

Both good, both successful, in conveying rejection

Different methods, tones, techniques (as shown)

YW means more to me as I can relate to the situation

Of course, your own plans don't need to be set out at such length. You can use abbreviations, diagrams, or whatever suits you. The plan is for your use only.

Here are two suggested ways you could plan your answer. Examiners value both equally.

Plan A is more straightforward and is used in the student plan opposite.

Plan B is more challenging because you have to juggle both poems in each paragraph.

Remember that the examiners will be looking for appropriate reference to texts. Jot down some short quotations when you make your plan, and include these when you write your answer.

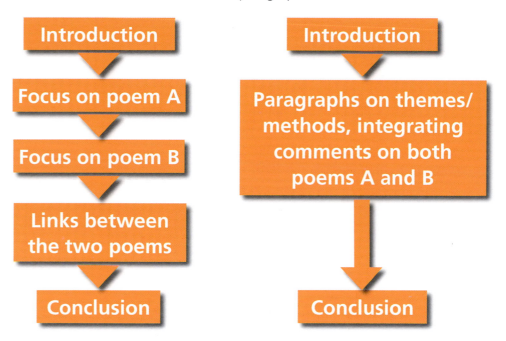

**Introduction**

**Focus on poem A**

**Focus on poem B**

**Links between the two poems**

**Conclusion**

**Introduction**

**Paragraphs on themes/ methods, integrating comments on both poems A and B**

**Conclusion**

**4** Read the question below. Using what you have learned, make a plan of your own. Take no more than 10 minutes. When you have finished, see how well you have done by using the checklist next to the plan opposite. If you can give yourself ticks all the way through, well done! If there is anything you would add or do differently, edit your plan.

Look again at *Hide and Seek* and *Brendon Gallacher*.

In what ways do the poets show the importance to children of the power of imagination?

In your answer you should make close reference to the language of the poems.

## EXAM TIP

In the exam there are two questions. You only need to answer one.

- Question 1 always names two poems.
- Question 2 names one poem and asks you to choose another suitable poem from the same section of the Anthology.

Ask yourself which one or two of the three poems named you know best. If you choose question 2, you will need to be sure that you can think of another suitable poem to write about.

For a good grade you need to write well about both poems in your answer. You also need to spend roughly an equal amount of time on each poem.

## 2 Write a clear opening

A good answer will start with a clear opening paragraph and then develop the points well.

Examiners want your opening paragraph to show:

- ☑ that you've thought about the form your whole answer will take before you get down to the details of the poems
- ☑ the direction your whole answer will take
- ☑ that both poems are going to be considered
- ☑ that the key words of the question are going to be addressed.

Examiners want your developing answer to:

- ☑ show evidence of planning in the use of paragraphs
- ☑ comment on the poems and show how well you understand them
- ☑ develop your points using quotations from the poems
- ☑ comment on how language is used in the poems right from the start.

> **5** Read the following openings of answers written by Student 1 and Student 2, and discuss the questions about them. You will then practise writing your own openings.

### Student 1

Which points in the checklist above does the introductory paragraph cover? Which are missing?

> In this essay I am going to write about two poems from the Edexcel Poetry Anthology, 'Refugee Blues' and 'You Will Be Hearing From Us Shortly'. They are both well-written, and I enjoyed them both very much. Both poems deal with rejection, and both are successful, but they use different methods. Rejection comes throughout 'Refugee Blues', e.g. 'Yet there's no place for us, my dear, yet there's no place for us' (line 3). There is also rejection in 'You Will Be Hearing From Us Shortly'.

From this opening, would an examiner feel that both poems are covered equally?

How could Student 1 improve the use of paragraphs to show clearly that the answer is addressing one point at a time?

> Once you get to line 7, though, you really begin to think that the person being interviewed is getting some bad treatment ('Not, we must admit, precisely what we had in mind'). The two poems develop in different ways as well. 'You Will be Hearing From Us Shortly' builds up slowly and steadily: the rejection begins on a small scale but gradually becomes a huge insult even of the person's right to existence.

Is the opening point about language in this paragraph well developed? How could you develop it to gain a higher mark? The highlighted text is an interesting point about language, but can you explain *why* the language gives an icy feeling?

> The rejection in this poem is expressed in very formal language, e.g. 'Would you care to defend their relevance?' ==This is true to the situation (an interview) and adds an icy sort of feeling to the effect of the poem.==

**Student 2**

Both poems deal with rejection, and both are successful, but they use different methods. 'Refugee Blues' deals with two people who represent a whole group of people and their experiences, whereas 'You Will Be Hearing From Us Shortly' concentrates on one individual.

==Rejection is clear as a theme in 'Refugee Blues' from the very start: 'Yet there's no place for us, my dear, yet there's no place for us' (line 3). In the first stanza, therefore, we are presented with the idea of two people with nowhere to stay. The repetition in the line brings out the importance of the feeling.== Rejection in 'You Will Be Hearing From Us Shortly' is not so immediately apparent. It isn't until half way through the second stanza that we really sense that the person being interviewed is getting some bad treatment ('Not, we must admit, precisely what we had in mind').

The two poems also differ slightly in the way they develop the theme of rejection. 'You Will Be Hearing From Us Shortly' builds up slowly and steadily: the interviewer's rejecting comments gather in power and rudeness until the huge insult of 'And you were born – ? Yes. Pity.' at the conclusion. By contrast, 'Refugee Blues' consists of a series of separate examples of the couple's rejection. It is the accumulation of these examples that gives the poem its impact, but there doesn't seem to be a narrative as such.

Look back to page 13, which describes two ways of planning an answer, A and B. Which method has Student 2 chosen?

This section uses PEC: point, evidence, comment. Is the next point about *You Will Be Hearing From Us Shortly* also well developed?

**6** Using what you have learnt, write an opening paragraph to the question below. Use your work on key words and planning to help you.

Look again at *Hide and Seek* and *Brendon Gallacher*.

In what ways do the poets show the importance to children of the power of imagination?

In your answer you should make close reference to the language of the poems.

**EXAM TIP**

If you're writing well-planned and well-written openings, you're on the way to writing good essays that will gain you higher marks.

**7** Test your opening using the checklist on page 12. How did you get on? If you can give yourself ticks all the way, well done! If there is anything you would do differently, edit your plan.

- 1st person (I, we, as in *Dulce et Decorum Est*)
- 2nd person (you, as in *You Will Be Hearing From Us Shortly*)
- 3rd person (he, she, it, they, as in *Half Past Two*).

## 3 Comment on the poets' use of language

Students who comment effectively on the way that poets use language will gain higher marks. Examiners want to see:

❖ your understanding of how poets use language to express thoughts and feelings and to create effects

❖ good references to the poems and use of quotations to illustrate your points

❖ follow-up comments, which develop your points and explain the purpose of the quotation.

## Understanding how poets use language

The 'language' of poetry means the words and phrases used by poets to create the exact meaning and effects they want. When you comment on a poet's words you should think about language features such as expression, sound effects, rhythm and pace, and tone.

> **1 Expression.** What individual words and phrases does the poet choose in order to make a point or express a feeling? Does the poet use descriptive terms? Why? Is there imagery, e.g. metaphors and similes? Why?

> **3 Sound effects.** Does the poet use sound effects such as rhyme, repetition, alliteration or assonance? Why?

> **2 Rhythm and pace.** Does the poem move quickly or slowly? Is there a regular rhythm, and what effect does this have? Are there contrasts in pace, and if so, how has the poet used them for particular purposes?

> **4 Tone.** What feelings are conveyed by the words, and how does the language convey this (e.g. formal or informal, serious or light-hearted)? Is there a single mood, or does it change? What voice is the poem written in (1st, 2nd, 3rd person)?

> **8** Read the extracts below from student essays on language features in *Dulce et Decorum Est* and *The Send-off*. Match each one to a language feature listed in the boxes above.

> **A** *There is a lot of emotive language in this poem, for example 'froth-corrupted lungs' and 'vile, incurable sores' and these all give it an intense feeling.*

> **B** *'Like old beggars under sacks' suggests that the young soldiers have aged and lost their vigour.*

> **C** *The rhythm of the line emphasises the central word 'silent' – they don't dare to speak of their experiences.*

> **D** *Although the use of assonance and cheerful rhyme in the words 'they sang their way' might make us expect something cheerful ...*

When you comment on language, remember to use the correct technical terms when appropriate, such as:

- **alliteration** (repeated consonant sounds), e.g. 's̲tood s̲taring hard'
- **assonance** (repeated vowel sounds), e.g. 'f̲umbling,/Fitting the cl̲umsy helmets'
- **enjambment** (when a phrase runs over into the next line), e.g. 'The blood/ Come gargling'
- **imagery** (the use of metaphor, simile or personification to draw a vivid picture), e.g. 'coughing like hags, we cursed through sludge'
- **onomatopoeia** (the sound of a word reflecting its meaning), e.g. 'sludge'.

Don't use these terms without commenting on their effect. Examiners call this 'feature spotting' and it will not get you any marks. Don't just say 'there is a simile in line 4', but explain what the effect of that simile is on the reader.

## Referring to the poems

When quotations are used well:

- ✓ they serve a purpose by illustrating a point
- ✓ the point is clearly explained
- ✓ they are not too long
- ✓ they are integrated into the candidate's own writing.

> **9** Read the extract from Student 1's essay below against the checklist above. Then read Student 2's work. Choose words from the poem extract provided above Student 2's work to complete the sentences.

**EXAM TIP**

Exam questions often ask you to 'focus on the poet's language' or 'pay close attention to the language of the poem'. Even when it does not state this directly, *always* comment on the poet's use of language in your answer. You could use REST to remember these features of poetic language:

**R**hythm and pace

**E**xpression

**S**ound effects

**T**one

**Student 1**

*The opening lines of the poem shock the reader. The images in the first two lines emphasise the physical state of the soldiers very effectively, as 'old beggars' makes us think of elderly men in a desperate state, not what we expect of young soldiers.*

**Student 2**

Gas! Gas! Quick, boys! – An ecstasy of fumbling,

Fitting the clumsy helmets just in time.

*The poet uses punctuation and a succession of short words '_____ _____' to convey the soldiers' panic when the gas shells explode. The adjective '_____' effectively describes their efforts to fit the awkward helmets which will save their lives.*

## Remember to
'flex your PECs' when commenting on language:

**P** – Point
**E** – Evidence
**C** – Comment

A good comment will improve your grade, because it shows (a) that you understand exactly how the poet has used language, and (b) that you are developing your interpretation of the poem.

# Developing your points on language

When you refer to a poem to make your point, don't leave it at that. Develop your point by making an additional comment showing how the quotation backs up your point. For example:

This is the main point that the student is making.

This is the evidence – quotes from the poem and reference to the poem.

The sound effects in *Dulce et Decorum Est* help the poet to paint a picture of the scene. For example, onomatopoeia is used in 'sludge' and 'trudge', the rhymes in lines 2 and 4. You can almost hear the soldiers dragging their feet out of the sticky mud with each painful step, and the rhyme emphasises this.

This is a further comment which shows in detail how the evidence supports the main point.

**10** These extracts from student essays all comment on the poet's language. They have been numbered in order of increasing effectiveness. Explain what makes each example better than the one before.

## Student 1

When the writer says that the soldiers were 'Bent double, like old beggars under sacks', it shows that the loads they were carrying must have been very heavy. There is alliteration in line 2.

## Student 2

The poem opens very dramatically, and we can easily picture the poor soldiers, as the similes are very effective. 'Bent double, like old beggars under sacks' gives us a clear visual picture of soldiers who are exhausted, carrying their heavy equipment.

## Student 3

Owen skilfully and economically establishes the atmosphere, and the condition of the soldiers, in the opening lines 'like old beggars under sacks'. The imagery seems chosen to contradict, or contrast with, the stereotype of the brave young soldier 'knock-kneed, coughing like hags', and this relates to the main theme of the poem.

## Student 4

The opening lines of the poem shock the reader, presenting a vivid picture of the soldiers' condition. The images in the first two lines emphasise their physical state very effectively, as 'old beggars' makes us think of elderly men in a desperate state, not what we expect of young soldiers. The alliteration of 'b' in line 1 and 'c' in line 2 adds the power of sound to the visual image.

**11** Read the sample essay opposite.

**(a)** Find two places where the student has developed the points by explaining the purpose of the quotation that has been used.

**(b)** The points that the student makes about the gas attack in the fifth paragraph could be improved. Using what you have learned, develop two of them in an effective way.

You are now going to pull together all the learning you have done in this unit by attempting a complete answer to a question on *The Send-off* and *Dulce et Decorum Est*. You will then study another student's answer for comparison.

**12 (a)** First answer the question below. You have 40 minutes.
   **(b)** Then read the student answer and examiner comments below. Complete the activities in the boxes.

Look again at *The Send-off* and *Dulce et Decorum Est*.

What impressions of war do these poems give, and what methods do the poets use to convey these impressions?

1   In 'The Send-off' it is obvious that the soldiers were not very keen on going off to fight in the war, all through the first three or four stanzas. The words 'faces grimly gay' indicate that the men didn't want to go but they kept their spirits up because they knew they had no choice. 'Grimly gay' is an oxymoron,
5   because you can't be grim and gay at the same time, and so it makes the reader think hard about their state of mind. When they returned from the war they seemed no happier than before, as we can see from the words 'many creep back, silent, to village wells'. The rhythm of the line emphasises the central word 'silent' – they don't dare to speak about their experiences.

10  The poem gives the impression that there were thousands of soldiers on the railway platform, and that they were all unhappy, or even scared, about going off to war. In stanza four they are sent off 'so secretly, like wrongs hushed up, they went'. This tells us that there were not happy thoughts, they were just sent away as quietly as possible. Also, when they came back (only
15  some of them), the poet writes 'A few, a few, too few for drums and yells, may creep back...' This indicates that when they returned from war there was no welcome home party. This is because too many of their comrades have died for there to be any celebration.

    There is a lot of descriptive language throughout the poem, such as the
20  opening line 'Down the close, darkening lanes they sang their way', and 'their breasts were stuck all white with wreath and spray'. Although the cheerful rhyme and the words 'they sang their way' might make us expect something cheerful, the mood soon changes with 'wreath', which is normally a word we think of to do with funerals.

There is no general introduction. Going straight into detail about one poem is not a good idea. Write bullet point notes on what you would include in the introduction.

How well has the student planned this answer? Look at the topics of the paragraphs. The first sentence will usually tell you what the paragraph is about.

Good answers:
☑ address the key words in the question
☑ develop some of the points
☑ comment on the poets' language right from the start

Look at the first three paragraphs with this checklist in mind. How well is this student doing?

There is some comment on the poet's use of language here, but it could be developed. How could you make more of the rhythm and rhyme in the first 5 lines of the poem to bring out the contrasts in mood?

25 In 'The Send-off' we do not actually see the soldiers on the battlefield, so the impression which the poem gives of the war is based only on their mood and expectations before they go to war ('grimly gay') and the terrible losses which they suffer ('a few, too few'). 'Dulce et Decorum Est', though, is actually set right in the battlefield, as the exhausted soldiers are trying to

30 get away from gas attacks, and the poem actually describes what it is like to be in the middle of a war.

For a start, we know that the soldiers were tired, ill and injured because in the first stanza it says 'knock-kneed, coughing like hags' and 'But limped on, bloodshod. All went lame, all blind;/Drunk with fatigue'. This gives us an insight

35 into what it was really like for them. The poor soldier who died in the gas attack because he did not get his helmet on in time died 'guttering, choking, drowning' and this memory still affects the poet. We know this because in the fourth stanza the poet writes that he still has nightmares about it. This is the true picture of war in this poem, and he gives us a dramatic and detailed account of

40 how the man died. He says 'Gas! Gas! Quick boys! – An ecstasy of fumbling' to show the panic when the gas attack starts, and he gives us a horrible picture of death – 'But someone still was yelling out and stumbling/And floundering like a man in fire or lime'. This is a simile.

There is a lot of emotive language in this poem, for example 'froth-corrupted

45 lungs' and 'vile incurable sore' and these all give it an intense feeling. The language contributes to the picture of somebody dying so hideously, and the traumatic effect it must have had on the person watching.

In conclusion I think that both poems give very negative impressions of war, and both do it very effectively. In 'The Send-off' the strongest impression comes

50 from how many soldiers died, so that only 'a few' came back, and in 'Dulce et Decorum Est' the strongest impression is of the terrible conditions, and the horror of the gas attack, described as if you were actually there yourself.

## The examiner's view

This response shows a very sound understanding of both poems, although the student has more to say about *Dulce et Decorum Est* than *The Send-off*. The comments on the poets' use of language are straightforward, and relevant to the question. There is interesting comment on the effects of language in places, but there are also examples where opportunities for further exploration are not taken. The quotations are appropriately chosen and well integrated into the answer, and worthwhile supporting comments are usually offered. The answer sticks to the question throughout.

**A low grade B**

13 Assess your own answer against this B grade answer. Look at the 'Steps to success in reading' on page 7 to check how well you are meeting the assessment objectives. What do you need to work on to improve your grade?

## 5 Exam question practice

Now is the time to put everything in this unit into practice for yourself.

**14** Allow 40 minutes, and choose one of the questions below. When you have finished, assess yourself against your answer to the question in Activity 12, or swap your work with your partner and assess each other's. Look back at the 'Steps to success in reading' on page 7 to identify exactly where you are doing well, and where you need to improve. Note down three areas in which you would like to improve, and practise those skills.

Remember that you cannot practise too much. Areas such as planning, writing good openings and ensuring that you comment on the poets' use of language will improve very quickly when you practise.

**1** Look again at *Where The Scattering Began* and ONE other poem from **In Such a Time as This** in which the poet looks at the experience of moving to a new country.

In what ways do the poets explore the challenges faced by those who have to adjust to a new way of life?

In your answer you should make close reference to the language of the poems.

*(Higher Tier)*

**2** Look again at *Electricity Comes To Cocoa Bottom* and *Wherever I Hang*. How does each poet create the mood and atmosphere of the place described?

**For** each poem you should comment on:

❖ the place which is being described
❖ the atmosphere which is created
❖ the use of language.

*(Foundation Tier)*

Remember to begin by thinking about the focus of the question. What are the key words? Then spend no more than a few minutes planning your answer.

**3** Look again at *Half-Past Two* and ONE other poem from **In Such a Time as This** which explores childhood experience. Discuss the ways in which the poets describe the thoughts and feelings of childhood.

In your answer you should make close reference to the language of the poems.

*(Higher Tier)*

**4** Look again at *Hide and Seek* and ONE other poem from **In Such a Time as This** which describes a memorable incident. How do the writers of these two poems help you to understand the events or incidents they describe?

For each poem you should write about:

❖ the details of the scene
❖ the feelings of the people
❖ the use of language.

*(Foundation Tier)*

## 1 Plan a balanced answer

Always read the question carefully and spend around 5–10 minutes planning your answer. First work out what the focus of the question is by noting the key words.

> 1 Read what an examiner says about the key words in the question below.

This is the focus of the question, the link between the two poems. There is always a focus – the question never says 'Write all you know about these two poems'!

This means you need to consider the poets' methods, the different techniques of language and verse they use to explore the topic.

Look back at *Not My Best Side* and *Once Upon a Time*.

Both poems deal with ==appearance and reality==. ==How do the two poets bring out these issues== through their writing?

In your answer you should make ==close reference to the language== of the poems.

You need to make interesting comments about how poets use language for effect, and support your comments with short quotations from the poems.

### EXAM TIP

Underline key words in the question in the exam and use them to help you plan. Use them throughout the essay, and at the end check back to make sure you have covered them in your answer. Foundation Tier questions will have bullet points to guide you in your answer. Make sure you write something on each of them.

> 2 Now read the following question. With a partner decide which are the key words and why. Then compare your ideas with others.

Look again at *Once Upon a Time* and *Still I Rise*.

How do the two poets deal with the setbacks and challenges which they have experienced in their lives?

In your answer you should make close reference to the language of the poems.

## Plan your answer

When you have highlighted your key words and got a firm grip on the question, you need to plan and shape your answer.

> 3 Read the student plan and examiner comments on the next page. You will use what you find out to write your own plan.

Look back at *Not My Best Side* and *Once Upon a Time*.

Both poems deal with <mark>appearance and reality</mark>. <mark>How</mark> do the two poets bring out these issues through their writing?

In your answer you should make <mark>close reference to the language</mark> of the poems

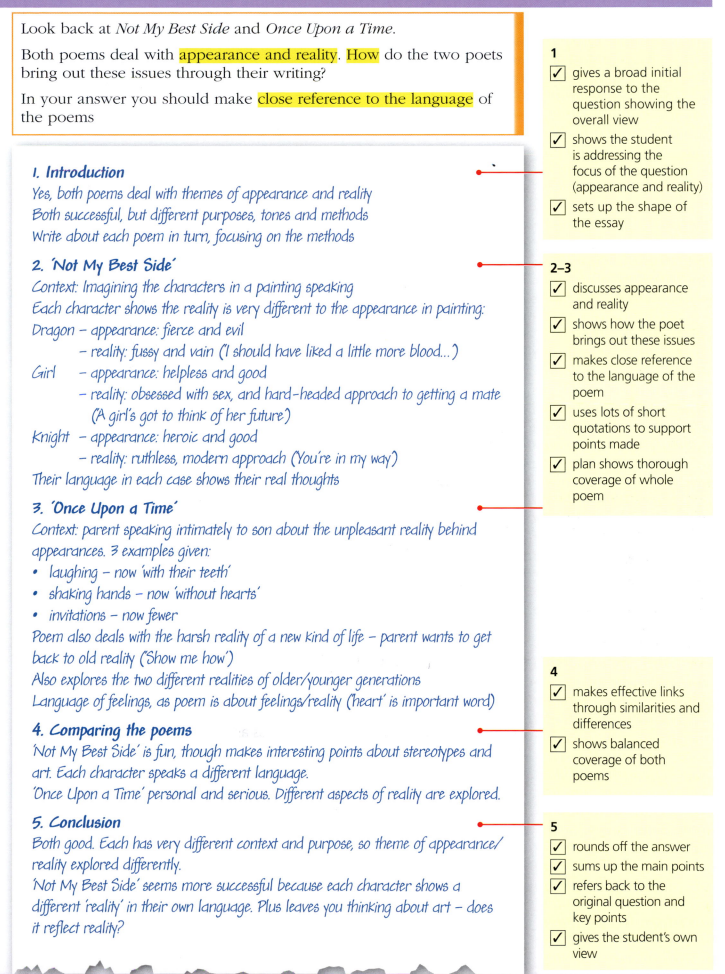

### 1. Introduction
Yes, both poems deal with themes of appearance and reality
Both successful, but different purposes, tones and methods
Write about each poem in turn, focusing on the methods

### 2. 'Not My Best Side'
Context: Imagining the characters in a painting speaking
Each character shows the reality is very different to the appearance in painting:
Dragon  – appearance: fierce and evil
     – reality: fussy and vain ('I should have liked a little more blood...')
Girl     – appearance: helpless and good
     – reality: obsessed with sex, and hard-headed approach to getting a mate
      ('A girl's got to think of her future')
Knight  – appearance: heroic and good
     – reality: ruthless, modern approach ('You're in my way')
Their language in each case shows their real thoughts

### 3. 'Once Upon a Time'
Context: parent speaking intimately to son about the unpleasant reality behind appearances. 3 examples given:
• laughing – now 'with their teeth'
• shaking hands – now 'without hearts'
• invitations – now fewer
Poem also deals with the harsh reality of a new kind of life – parent wants to get back to old reality ('Show me how')
Also explores the two different realities of older/younger generations
Language of feelings, as poem is about feelings/reality ('heart' is important word)

### 4. Comparing the poems
'Not My Best Side' is fun, though makes interesting points about stereotypes and art. Each character speaks a different language.
'Once Upon a Time' personal and serious. Different aspects of reality are explored.

### 5. Conclusion
Both good. Each has very different context and purpose, so theme of appearance/reality explored differently.
'Not My Best Side' seems more successful because each character shows a different 'reality' in their own language. Plus leaves you thinking about art – does it reflect reality?

**1**
- ✓ gives a broad initial response to the question showing the overall view
- ✓ shows the student is addressing the focus of the question (appearance and reality)
- ✓ sets up the shape of the essay

**2–3**
- ✓ discusses appearance and reality
- ✓ shows how the poet brings out these issues
- ✓ makes close reference to the language of the poem
- ✓ uses lots of short quotations to support points made
- ✓ plan shows thorough coverage of whole poem

**4**
- ✓ makes effective links through similarities and differences
- ✓ shows balanced coverage of both poems

**5**
- ✓ rounds off the answer
- ✓ sums up the main points
- ✓ refers back to the original question and key points
- ✓ gives the student's own view

Of course, your own plans don't need to be set out at such length. You can use abbreviations, diagrams, or whatever suits you. The plan is for your use only.

There are two ways you could plan your answer. Examiners value both equally.

Plan A is more straightforward and is used in the student plan on page 23.

used in the student plan on page 23.

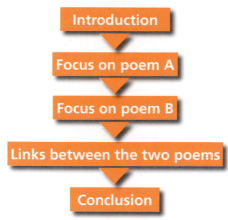

Plan B is more challenging because you have to juggle both poems in each paragraph.

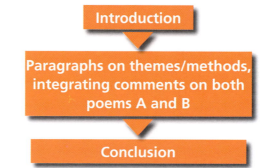

4 Read the question below. Using what you have learned, make a plan of your own. Take no more than 10 minutes. When you have finished, check how well you have done by using the checklist next to the plan on page 23. If you can give yourself ticks all the way through, well done! If there is anything you would do differently, edit your plan.

Look again at *Warning* and *I Shall Paint My Nails Red*. What impressions have you formed of the characters in these two poems?

In your answer you should make close reference to the language of the poems.

---

**Remember**, that the examiners will be looking for appropriate reference to texts. Jot down some short quotations when you make your plan, and include these when you write your answer.

**EXAM TIP**

In the exam there are two questions. You only need to answer one.

- Question 1 always names two poems.
- Question 2 names one poem and asks you to choose another suitable poem from the same section of the Anthology.

Ask yourself which one or two of the three poems named you know best. If you choose question 2, you will need to be sure that you can think of another suitable poem to write about.

For a good grade you need to write well about both poems in your answer. You also need to spend roughly an equal amount of time on each poem.

## 2 Write a clear opening

A good answer will start with a clear opening paragraph and then develop the points well.

Examiners want your introduction to show:

- [✓] that you've thought about your whole answer before you get down to details
- [✓] the direction your whole answer will take
- [✓] that both poems are going to be considered
- [✓] that the key words of the question are going to be addressed.

Examiners want your developing answer to:

- [✓] show evidence of planning in the use of paragraphs
- [✓] comment on the poems and show how well you understand them
- [✓] develop your points using quotations from the poems
- [✓] comment on how language is used in the poems right from the start.

*Remember*, a well-planned introduction is a short and useful opening paragraph. A well-planned conclusion may also be just one paragraph.

> **5** Read the following openings of answers written by Student 1 and Student 2, and discuss the questions about them. You will then practise writing your own openings.

### Student 1

Does the opening of this essay show evidence of planning? If not, can you give the student some detailed advice? (Hint: look at Student 2's answer.)

I think that 'Not My Best Side' is best where the girl, who is like the maiden in an old fairy story, talks to the dragon. The dragon is obviously worried about his appearance a lot, and in fact he is the one who says the words that make up the poem's title. Also the knight on the picture, who is St George, is very conscious of his appearance, and proud of his spear and armour, saying that they are both 'still on the secret list', and he seems to think that he deserves to get the girl just because he is so modern and well turned out. Also 'Once Upon a Time' talks about pretending when he says he has learnt to wear different faces: 'homeface, officeface, streetface, hostface, cocktailface', and the man who is giving the message to his son seems to feel that appearances now count for more than the truth. This is like the maiden in the other poem, when she says 'What was he like underneath the hardware?'.

The student launches straight into a detailed discussion of the poems. Why is this not the best way to start?

What points in the checklist above does the introduction cover? Which are missing?

How could Student 1 develop the highlighted quotation? Explain what is meant by this list of faces.

Which of the key words of the question does Student 2 focus on in the introductory paragraph?

Student 2 could gain marks by commenting on the language of the poems from the start. What could you add to back up the point about the different tone of each poem (paragraph 2) by referring to the poets' use of language? For example, where is the evidence that the older man's tone is 'quite sad and bitter'?

**Student 2**

Appearance and reality are the issues at the centre of both poems. However, the ways in which the poets present these ideas are very different.

In 'Not My Best Side', the poet brings out the gap between appearance and reality in a light-hearted, humorous way, bringing to life the three characters in a famous painting. In 'Once Upon a Time', a father is talking to his son about how people used to be sincere and genuine in their dealings with each other, but now he feels that many people are hypocrites. The older man's tone is quite sad and bitter, and he tells his son that he has forgotten how to laugh.

As well as contrasting in tone, the two poems also differ in the way they use language and poetic techniques. In 'Not My Best Side', the issue of appearance, and how we naturally want to be seen at our best, is brought out in the title itself. These words are repeated by the dragon at the start of the poem...

Look back to page 24 which describes two ways of planning an answer, A and B. Which method has Student 2 chosen?

From this opening, would an examiner feel that both poems are going to be covered equally?

**6** Using what you have learnt, write the opening paragraph of an answer to the question below. Use your work on key words and planning to help you.

Look again at *Warning* and *I Shall Paint My Nails Red*. What impressions have you formed of the characters in these two poems?

In your answer you should make close reference to the language of the poems.

## EXAM TIP

If you're writing well-planned and well-written openings, you're on the way to writing good essays that will gain you higher marks.

**7** Test your opening using the checklist on page 25. How did you get on? If you can give yourself ticks all the way, well done! If there is anything you would do differently, edit your plan.

# 3 Comment on the poets' use of language

Students who comment effectively on the way that poets use language will gain higher marks. Examiners want to see:

❖ your understanding of how poets use language to express thoughts and feelings and to create effects

❖ good references to the poems and use of quotations to illustrate your points

❖ follow-up comments, which develop your points and explain the purpose of the quotation.

## Understanding how poets use language

The 'language' of poetry means the words and phrases used by poets to create the exact meaning and effects they want. When you comment on a poet's words you should think about language features such as expression, sound effects, rhythm and pace, and tone.

*Remember*, 'voice' means the speaker of the poem. It might, for example, be the poet writing about other people; it might be the poet pretending to be someone else. There are three main voices:

• 1st person (I, we, as in *Mid Term Break*)

• 2nd person (you, as in *Still I Rise*)

• 3rd person (he, she, it, they, as in *Follower*)

---

**1 Expression.** What individual words and phrases does the poet choose in order to make a point or express a feeling? Does the poet use descriptive terms? Why? Is there imagery, e.g. metaphors and similes? Why?

**3 Sound effects.** Does the poet use sound effects such as rhyme, repetition, alliteration or assonance? Why?

**2 Rhythm and pace.** Does the poem move quickly or slowly? Is there a regular rhythm, and what effect does this have? Are there contrasts in pace, and if so, how has the poet used them for particular purposes?

**4 Tone.** What feelings are conveyed by the words, and how does the language convey this (e.g. formal or informal, serious or light-hearted)? Is there a single mood, or does it change? What voice is the poem written in (1st, 2nd, 3rd person)?

---

**8** Read the extracts below from student essays on language features in *Mid-Term Break* and *The Barn*. Match each one to a language feature listed in the boxes above.

**A** A menacing and frightening atmosphere is built up ... in stanza 2 we read of the 'mouse-grey, smooth, chilly concrete'.

**B** The young Heaney 'scuttled fast into the sunlit yard', where the metaphor suggests he is like a small insect.

**C** The easy rhythm of the poem helps to carry the narrative along, and sets up a poignant contrast with the difficulty being described.

**D** The sound of line 10 'A scythe's edge, a clean spade, a pitch-fork's prongs' where the clash of consonants makes the words move slowly but fiercely, like lumbering ghosts.

Exam questions often ask you to 'focus on the poet's language' or 'pay close attention to the language of the poem'. Even when it does not state this directly, *always* comment on the poet's use of language in your answer. You could use REST to remember these features of poetic language:

**R**hythm and pace

**E**xpression

**S**ound effects

**T**one

When you comment on language, remember to use the correct technical terms when appropriate, such as:

❖ **alliteration** (repeated consonant sounds), e.g. '<u>s</u>olid as <u>c</u>ement in two-lugged <u>s</u>acks'

❖ **assonance** (repeated vowel sounds), e.g. 'He lay in the four foot b<u>o</u>x as in his c<u>o</u>t'

❖ **enjambment** (when a phrase runs over into the next line), e.g. 'I saw him/ For the first time in six weeks'

❖ **imagery** (the use of metaphor, simile or personification to draw a vivid picture), e.g. 'The two-lugged sacks moved in like great blind rats'

❖ **onomatopoeia** (the sound of a word reflecting its meaning), e.g. 'the baby cooed'.

Don't use these terms without commenting on their effect. Examiners call this 'feature spotting' and it will not get you any marks. Don't just say 'there is a simile in line 4', but explain what the effect of that simile is on the reader.

## Referring to the poems

When quotations are used well:

☑ they serve a purpose by illustrating a point

☑ the point is clearly explained

☑ they are not too long

☑ they are integrated into the candidate's own writing.

> **9** Read the extract from Student 1's essay below against the checklist above. Then read Student 2's work. Choose words from the poem extract provided above Student 2's work to complete the sentences.

### Student 1

*We can sense a tension which the poet is feeling, as he is 'counting bells', waiting for 'classes' to come 'to a close'. Time is clearly moving very slowly for him.*

### Student 2

The baby cooed and laughed and rocked the pram

When I came in, and I was embarrassed

By old men standing up to shake my hand

*The poet expresses the baby's lack of awareness of the grim atmosphere by describing how it '_____' and '_____'.*
*The mixture of emotions the boy experiences is shown when he is '_____' that old men show him unusual respect.*

# Developing your points on language

When you refer to a poem to make your point, don't leave it at that. Develop your point by making an additional comment showing how the quotation backs up your point. For example:

This is the main point that the student is making.

This is the evidence – a reference to the poem (here an actual quotation).

> Heaney also describes his environment very convincingly in 'The Barn'. At night we are told that 'The dark gulfed like a roof space'. This reminds us that he is still young, seeing everything in a childlike perspective, so that everything seems bigger to him.

This is a further comment which shows in detail how the evidence supports the main point.

**Remember** to 'flex your PECs' when commenting on language:

**P** – Point
**E** – Evidence
**C** – Comment

A good comment will improve your grade, because it shows (a) that you understand exactly how the poet has used language, and (b) that you are developing your interpretation of the poem.

**10** These extracts from student essays all comment on the poet's language. They have been numbered in order of increasing effectiveness. Explain what makes each example better than the one before.

## Student 1

Heaney shows excellent command of language in this poem. Note especially the alliteration, assonance and metaphor in 'Then you felt cobwebs clogging up your lungs/And scuttled fast into the sunlit yard'.

## Student 2

The young poet met some cobwebs and then 'scuttled fast into the sunlit yard'. He was frightened by all the objects in the dark barn, which is why he was scuttling. The scuttling makes him like a little spider himself.

## Student 3

The young person in the poem is compared to a spider ('scuttled'), a good comparison as he probably felt small at the time and scuttling is what spiders do and also there would have been spiders in the barn. In fact he is running from cobwebs – another connection.

## Student 4

All these images explain why the young Heaney 'scuttled fast into the sunlit yard', where the metaphor suggests he is like a small insect, or a spider – tiny, perhaps afraid, perhaps moving without obvious direction. The speed of his 'escape', reinforced by the rhythm of the line, suggests that he is petrified of what he has left behind in the barn.

**11** Read the sample essay opposite. Identify two places where the student has done each of the following:

**(a)** linked the points with well-chosen quotations

**(b)** developed the points in detail with reference to the language of the poet.

## 4 Work with student answers

You are now going to pull together all the learning you have done in this section by attempting a complete essay answer to a question on *Mid-Term Break* and *The Barn*. You will then study another student's answer for comparison.

**12** **(a)** First answer the question below. You have 40 minutes.
**(b)** Then read the student answer and examiner comments below. Complete the activities in the boxes.

> Look again at *Mid-Term Break* and *The Barn*. Each describes an event or activity which made a lasting impression on the poet.
>
> In what ways does each poem bring this event or activity to life?
>
> In your answer you should make close reference to the language of the poems.

What makes this a good introduction? Look back at the checklist on page 25.

**1** 'Mid–Term Break' is clearly a poem in which the events described had a traumatic and lasting effect on the poet, and the poem has great poignancy as we read it today. Another Seamus Heaney poem, 'The Barn', also deals with events which left a lasting impression, although here the emotion is less **5** blunt and the events described are less dramatic, at least to an outsider.

Good answers:
- [✓] address the key words in the question
- [✓] develop some of the points
- [✓] comment on the poets' language right from the start

Look at the first three paragraphs with this checklist in mind. How well is this student doing?

Although 'Mid–Term Break' may initially suggest a sense of detachment, as the child narrator is away from home 'I sat all morning in the college sick bay', Heaney's intense yet economical use of language makes it clear to the reader very quickly that death, and the emotions surrounding it, are at the **10** heart of this poem. No time or space is wasted on establishing a context to the events, and we are drawn in to share the narrator's involvement in the action; the easy rhythm of the poem helps to carry the narrative along, and sets up a poignant contrast with the difficulty being described.

The later events in the poem are foreshadowed by 'knelling', in line 2, a **15** word we cannot help associating with funerals and death, as this is before we have any idea of the main event in the poem. As well as this specific sense of anticipation we can sense a tension which the poet is feeling, as he is 'counting bells', waiting for 'classes' to come 'to a close'. Time is clearly

Integrating quotations into your sentences is the best way of referring to the text. How has the student used quotations to explain and back up the points made? Why do you think this works well?

moving very slowly for him, as he worries about what is to come. Even the **20** venue of his wait, 'the college sick bay', contributes to the feelings of worry and to his sense of some impending misfortune. However the first real indication we get that something has gone horribly wrong is when we are told that 'our neighbours drove' him home: why couldn't his father come for him?

**25** The emotions which have so far been hinted at, or foretold, are now made explicit. The young Heaney writes 'in the porch I met my father crying' and this has an immediate impact on him.

The poet's sparse, simple description gives the moment its impact, as we are left to reflect on the range of emotions – shock, confusion – which Heaney may be feeling.

We then learn that his father 'had always taken funerals in his stride' and we also meet Big Jim Evans 'saying it was a hard blow'. The fact that these men, normally considered so strong and resilient (Big Jim Evans), and who do not easily show emotion, are so much affected by what has happened reinforces the idea in both Heaney's and the reader's mind that something dreadful must have happened. We can fully appreciate why the event had such significance for the poet, and made such a lasting impression – and yet we have still to be told the precise nature of the event itself.

Strongly felt emotion, experienced at first hand by the poet and conveyed to the reader in the first person, is also a feature of 'The Barn'. Here we are made to understand, if not to share, the feelings of fear which Heaney experienced as a child. A menacing and frightening atmosphere is built up from the very start of the poem, especially in stanza two when we read of the 'mouse-grey, smooth, chilly concrete' which seems to have an almost repulsive quality to it, as though it almost has a malign personality of its own. As the poem moves on Heaney's fear intensifies. We are told that there were 'no windows' and that there was only one door which 'meant no draughts': this seems to emphasise the feeling of imprisonment – cells have no windows and only one door, perhaps. If the one door is blocked, there is no escape. The feeling of claustrophobia is reinforced by the sound of line 10 ('A scythe's edge, a clean spade, a pitchfork's prongs'), where the clash of consonants make the words move slowly but fiercely, like lumbering ghosts. All these images explain why the young Heaney 'scuttled fast into the sunlit yard', where the metaphor suggests he is like a small insect, or a spider – tiny, afraid, perhaps moving without obvious direction. The speed of his 'escape', reinforced by the rhythm of the line, suggests that he is petrified of what he has left behind in the barn.

As with 'Mid-Term Break', Heaney has made the emotions which he felt at the time seem important and significant in themselves: the intensity of the emotion and how it has been recreated stands almost independently of the context and the narrative. However, Heaney does give us a clear picture of the events and the background, in both poems, and these add to the overall way in which the events are brought to life.

As events unfold in 'Mid-Term Break', we again see a conflict of emotions. As he learns what has happened, Heaney as a young boy is 'embarrassed/By old men standing up to shake my hand'. He also tells us that 'his mother held my hand' which, as he would normally consider himself too grown up to be doing that, re-emphasises his desperation and the depth of his emotion. His mother on the other hand (and it is interesting to note how the bulk of the poem, about the narrator's own feelings, contrasts with description of others' emotions) seems to be grieving quietly: in fact the emotion which she does express is anger, rather than simple grief, in the line (she) 'coughed out angry tearless sighs'. The description of the central event is never explicit, until very near the end 'the bumper knocked him clear' and so, for the reader, there is even an element of surprise – what actually happened? – in amongst the other emotions which we observe. At times Heaney's writing can seem a little brutal, or deliberately

This is one example of where the student comments cleverly on the poet's use of language with quotations to support. Can you find another example in this paragraph?

This answer is organised by theme, rather than by poem. How does the student show which poem is being referred to at every point?

The student's understanding of the poet's language and how he uses it for effect is one of the great strengths of this essay. Find two examples of this feature of the essay in this paragraph.

impersonal – 'the ambulance arrived/with the corpse' rather than 'body' for example; but this deliberate coldness or objectivity, only tends to heighten the rest of this very emotional poem. Heaney also makes effective use of symbols, and of images which have strong associations, at the end of the poem. For example 'snowdrops/And candles soothed his bedside' – purity, innocence, the atmosphere of a church or an altar; or 'Wearing a poppy bruise', the symbol of remembrance. Overall, we are given a clear picture of the whole scene, and we understand fully why it was so significant for the youthful poet.

Heaney also describes his environment very convincingly in 'The Barn'. At night we are told that 'The dark gulfed like a roof space'. This reminds us that he is still young, seeing everything in a childlike perspective, so that everything seems bigger to him. In the same stanza we discover that even though he has physically left the barn, he cannot escape from it mentally, as nightmares about 'great blind rats' plague his dreams. Another skilful recreation of the child's frame of mind can be seen in the frightening personification of 'two lugged sacks moved in' to threaten him. Fear, and dreadful anticipation, are common to both poems.

It could perhaps even be said that Heaney is, in these two poems, revisiting aspects of his childhood that he may wish he could forget – or, perhaps, writing down an account of these traumas may have helped him to accept them. The vivid accounts and strong emotions which he conjures up certainly bring the events to life in dramatic ways, and the density of his language is the means by which he achieves this. He draws the reader into each experience very effectively, letting the reader share all the emotions and reactions as they occur: this is how the events are brought to life.

> How well has the student concluded the essay? Does the ending refer to any of the key words in the question? Does it sum up the student's view?

## The examiner's view

This is an excellent answer. Coverage of both poems is good, and the candidate shows awareness of the question at all times. The comments on the poet's language are penetrating, with some sophisticated evaluation of poetic effects. References to the poems are always purposeful, and ideas are frequently explored in a confident and original way. The essay is a coherent and very fluently expressed response to the question as a whole.

**A grade A\***

**13** Assess your own answer against this A\* grade answer. Look at the 'Steps to success in reading' on page 7 to check how well you are meeting the assessment objectives. What do you need to work on to improve your grade?

Now is the time to put everything in this unit into practice for yourself.

**Remember** that you cannot practise too much. Areas such as planning, writing good openings and ensuring that you comment on the poets' use of language will improve very quickly when you practise.

**14** Allow 40 minutes, and choose one of the questions below. When you have finished, assess yourself against your answer to the question in Activity 12, or swap your work with your partner and assess each other's. Look back at the 'Steps to success in reading' on page 7 to identify where you are doing well and where you need to improve. Note down three areas in which you would like to improve, and practise those skills.

1   Look again at *Old Man, Old Man* and ONE other poem from **Identity** in which the poet looks at the experience of being old.

In what ways do the poets explore the contrasts between different stages in a person's life?

In your answer you should make close reference to the language of the poems.

*(Higher Tier)*

2   Look again at *An Unknown Girl* and *I Shall Paint My Nails Red*.

What do we learn from these two poems about what the poets think and feel about decorating their hands or nails?

For each poem you should comment on:
   ❖ why each poet chooses to have her hands or nails painted
   ❖ the importance to the poet of the colour or pattern
   ❖ the other people mentioned in each poem
   ❖ the way the poets use language.

*(Foundation Tier)*

**Remember** to begin by thinking about the focus of the question. What are the key words? Then spend no more than a few minutes planning your answer.

3   Look again at *Follower* and *Digging*. Compare the poet's attitude to his father and grandfather, and the methods he uses to describe it.

In your answer you should make close reference to the language of the poems.

*(Higher Tier)*

4   Look again at *Death of a Naturalist* and ONE other poem from **Identity** which describes an important experience in a person's early life. Discuss the ways in which the poets describe the thoughts and feelings of the child.

For each poem you should comment on:
   ❖ how the experience affected the child
   ❖ how the language of the poems is used to show the thoughts and feelings
   ❖ any similarities or differences between the poems.

*(Foundation Tier)*

# 1 Plan a balanced answer

Always read the question carefully and spend around 5–10 minutes planning your answer. First work out what the focus of the question is by noting the key words.

**1** Read what an examiner says about the key words in the question below.

This is the focus of the question, the link between the two poems. There is always a focus – the question never says 'Write all you know about these two poems'!

## EXAM TIP

Underline key words when you read the question in the exam and use them to help you plan. Use them throughout the essay and at the end check back to make sure you have covered the main areas in your answer. Foundation Tier questions will have bullet points to guide you in your answer. Make sure that you write something about each bullet point.

Look again at *The Thought-Fox* and *A Blade of Grass*.

Write about the different ways in which the writers explore the ==link between nature and the writing of poetry==.

In your answer you should make ==close reference to the language== of the poems.

You need to make interesting comments about how poets use language for effect, and support your comments with short quotations from the poems.

**2** Now read the following question. With a partner decide which are the key words and why. Then compare your ideas with others.

Look again at *Iguana Memory* and *Roe-Deer*. In both poems human beings and animals meet.

How does each poem convey the nature and significance of these meetings?

In your answer you should make close reference to the language of the poems.

## Plan your answer

When you have highlighted your key words and got a firm grip on the question, you need to plan and shape your answer.

**3** Read the student plan and examiner comments on the next page. You will use what you find out to write your own plan.

Look again at *The Thought-Fox* and *A Blade of Grass*.

Write about the different ways in which the writers explore the <mark>link between nature and the writing of poetry</mark>.

In your answer you should make <mark>close reference to the language</mark> of the poems.

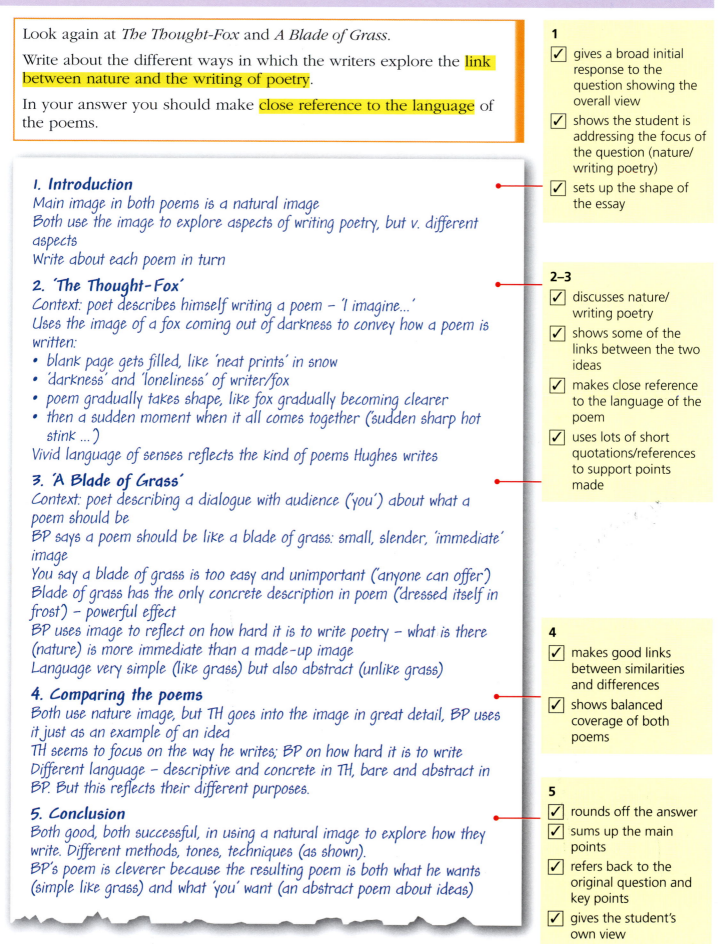

### 1. Introduction
Main image in both poems is a natural image
Both use the image to explore aspects of writing poetry, but v. different aspects
Write about each poem in turn

### 2. 'The Thought-Fox'
Context: poet describes himself writing a poem – 'I imagine...'
Uses the image of a fox coming out of darkness to convey how a poem is written:
* blank page gets filled, like 'neat prints' in snow
* 'darkness' and 'loneliness' of writer/fox
* poem gradually takes shape, like fox gradually becoming clearer
* then a sudden moment when it all comes together ('sudden sharp hot stink ...')
Vivid language of senses reflects the kind of poems Hughes writes

### 3. 'A Blade of Grass'
Context: poet describing a dialogue with audience ('you') about what a poem should be
BP says a poem should be like a blade of grass: small, slender, 'immediate' image
You say a blade of grass is too easy and unimportant ('anyone can offer')
Blade of grass has the only concrete description in poem ('dressed itself in frost') – powerful effect
BP uses image to reflect on how hard it is to write poetry – what is there (nature) is more immediate than a made-up image
Language very simple (like grass) but also abstract (unlike grass)

### 4. Comparing the poems
Both use nature image, but TH goes into the image in great detail, BP uses it just as an example of an idea
TH seems to focus on the way he writes; BP on how hard it is to write
Different language – descriptive and concrete in TH, bare and abstract in BP. But this reflects their different purposes.

### 5. Conclusion
Both good, both successful, in using a natural image to explore how they write. Different methods, tones, techniques (as shown).
BP's poem is cleverer because the resulting poem is both what he wants (simple like grass) and what 'you' want (an abstract poem about ideas)

**1**
- ✓ gives a broad initial response to the question showing the overall view
- ✓ shows the student is addressing the focus of the question (nature/writing poetry)
- ✓ sets up the shape of the essay

**2–3**
- ✓ discusses nature/writing poetry
- ✓ shows some of the links between the two ideas
- ✓ makes close reference to the language of the poem
- ✓ uses lots of short quotations/references to support points made

**4**
- ✓ makes good links between similarities and differences
- ✓ shows balanced coverage of both poems

**5**
- ✓ rounds off the answer
- ✓ sums up the main points
- ✓ refers back to the original question and key points
- ✓ gives the student's own view

Of course, your own plans don't need to be set out at such length. You can use abbreviations, diagrams, or whatever suits you. The plan is for your use only.

Here are two suggested ways you could plan your answer. Examiners value both equally.

Plan A is more straightforward and is used in the student plan on page 35.

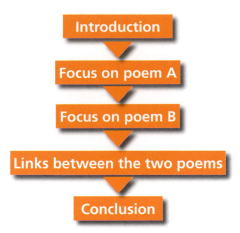

Plan B is more challenging because you have to juggle both poems in each paragraph.

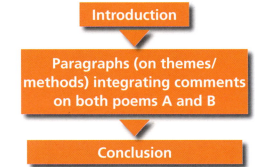

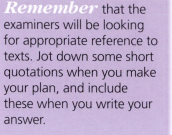

***Remember*** that the examiners will be looking for appropriate reference to texts. Jot down some short quotations when you make your plan, and include these when you write your answer.

## EXAM TIP

In the exam there are two questions. You only need to answer one.

- Question 1 always names two poems.
- Question 2 names one poem and asks you to choose another suitable poem from the same section of the Anthology.

Ask yourself which one or two of the three poems mentioned you know best. If you choose question 2, you will need to be sure that you can think of another suitable poem to write about.

For a good grade you need to write well about both poems in your answer. You also need to spend roughly an equal amount of time on each poem.

4 Read the question below. Using what you have learned, make a plan of your own. Take no more than 10 minutes. When you have finished, check how well you have done by using the checklist next to the plan on page 35. If you can give yourself ticks all the way through, well done! If there is anything you would do differently, edit your plan.

Look again at *Thistles* and *Nettles*. What do you learn from each poem about the writer's view of nature?

In your answer you should make close reference to the language of the poems.

## 2 Write a clear opening

A good answer will start with a clear opening paragraph and then develop the points well.

Examiners want your introduction to show:

☑ that you've thought about your whole answer before you get down to details

☑ the direction your whole answer will take

☑ that both poems are going to be considered

☑ that the key words of the question are going to be addressed.

Examiners want your developing answer to:

☑ show evidence of planning in the use of paragraphs

☑ comment on the poems and show how well you understand them

☑ develop your points using quotations from the poems

☑ comment on how language is used in the poems right from the start.

*Remember*, a well-planned introduction is short and useful and may be just one paragraph. A well-planned conclusion may also be just one paragraph.

> **5** Read the following openings of answers written by Student 1 and Student 2, and discuss the questions about them. You will then practise writing your own openings.

**Student 1**

Which points in the first checklist above does the intoductory paragraph cover? Which are missing?

Ted Hughes describes how a fox slowly comes out of the darkness and becomes clearer and more vivid to the writer. The fox begins in the darkness, then small details are mentioned one at a time – the nose, the eyes, the footprints – which is an excellent way of describing how an animal gradually emerges from the undergrowth.

Brian Patten has a very different approach. His poem is like a dialogue between the poet and someone else ('you' is the first word), it isn't clear who he is talking to. They are arguing about what makes a poem. There is a lot of toing and froing, as 'I' (Brian Patten) says one thing and 'you' say another. This is very different from Ted Hughes, who is on his own.

In both of these poems, however, the poets use nature to discuss and explore different aspects of writing poetry. They have different things to say about writing poetry, so the discussion is very different in each case. And they use different images – a fox and a blade of grass.

How does Student 1 show clearly that each of the first two paragraphs is addressing a different poem?

From this opening, would an examiner feel that both poems are covered equally?

Does Student 1 show the ability to comment on the poet's language? If not, how could you improve the first paragraph? Where, for example, could you use a quotation effectively?

Which points in the checklist on page 37 does the introductory paragraph cover?

Look back to page 36 which describes two ways of planning an answer, A and B. Which method has Student 2 chosen?

In paragraph 2 the student makes a point about the structure of the poem. Structure in a poem refers to the order in which things are described, and the way the lines are organised into groups or verses. Is this point about structure well developed in your view? Give reasons for your answer.

This answer shows that Student 2 can comment on the language of the poems in some detail. Where in the third paragraph could Student 2 have used a quotation to good effect?

## EXAM TIP

If you're writing well-planned and well-written openings, you're on the way to writing good essays that will gain you higher marks.

**Student 2**

In both of these poems the poets use an image from nature to discuss and explore different aspects of writing poetry. Their precise purpose, and the direction their thoughts take them, make this discussion very different in each case. I will explore each poem in turn before considering the connections between the two.

Ted Hughes describes how a fox slowly comes out of the darkness and becomes clearer and more vivid to the writer. So the bulk of the poem is the kind of compelling and detailed description of nature that we expect from this poet. However, the careful structure of the poem shows us that the poet has another purpose: he begins by picturing himself at a particular time and place, with a blank page before him, and he ends by referring to the same place (note the repetition of the 'window' and 'clock') but with the poem now written ('the page is printed'). This structure adds an extra dimension to the poem.

As we read the poem, therefore, we are on the lookout for the connection between writing a poem and the fox. To begin with, the poet makes it clear that this incident is in his mind ('I imagine' in line 1; and even before that, the strange title alerts us to the fact that this is no ordinary fox). So he is saying that here is a description of how his imagination works. Yet it is also very vivid: the details in stanza 3 onwards make it appear that the fox is really there. For the poet, he is!

**6** Using what you have learnt, write the opening paragraph of an answer to the question to the question below. Use your work on key words and planning to help you.

Look again at *Thistles* and *Nettles*. What do you learn from each poem about the writer's view of nature?

In your answer you should make close reference to the language of the poems.

**7** Test your opening using the checklist on page 37. How did you get on? If you can give yourself ticks all the way, well done! If there is anything you would do differently, edit your plan.

# 3 Comment on the poets' use of language

Students who understand and comment effectively on the way that poets use language will gain higher marks. Examiners want to see:

- your understanding of how poets use language to express thoughts and feelings and to create effects
- good references to the poems and use of quotations to illustrate your points
- follow-up comments, which develop your points and explain the purpose of the quotation.

## Understanding how poets use language

The 'language' of poetry means the words and phrases used by poets to create the exact meaning and effects they want. When you comment on a poet's words you should think about language features such as expression, sound effects, rhythm and pace, and tone.

> *Remember*, 'voice' means the speaker of the poem. It might, for example, be the poet writing about other people; it might be the poet pretending to be someone else. There are three main voices:
>
> - 1st person (I, we, as in *The Thought-Fox*)
> - 2nd person (you, as in *A Blade of Grass*)
> - 3rd person (he, she, it, they, as in *Trout*)

1 **Expression.** What individual words and phrases does the poet choose in order to make a point or express a feeling? Does the poet use descriptive terms? Why? Is there imagery, e.g. metaphors and similes? Why?

3 **Sound effects.** Does the poet use sound effects such as rhyme, repetition, alliteration or assonance? Why?

2 **Rhythm and pace.** Does the poem move quickly or slowly? Is there a regular rhythm, and what effect does this have? Are there contrasts in pace, and if so, how has the poet used them for particular purposes?

4 **Tone.** What feelings are conveyed by the words, and how does the language convey this (e.g. formal or informal, serious or light-hearted)? Is there a single mood, or does it change? What voice is the poem written in (1st, 2nd, 3rd person)?

8 Read the extracts below from student essays on language features in *Iguana Memory* and *Roe-Deer*. Match each one to a language feature listed in the boxes above.

A ... the first line, which sounds like a child's casual conversation in tone: 'saw an iguana once'..

B The made-up word 'newleaf' is very effective, and just brings out how vivid and full of life the iguana was, to this young girl, as well as suggesting a particular shade of bright green.

C ...the pause between 'hurrying' and the final line cleverly suggesting the moment before it scurried off.

D The two hyphenated expressions 'dawn-dirty' and 'blue-dark deer' are strongly alliterative to emphasise the importance of the encounter.

## EXAM TIP

Exam questions often ask you to 'focus on the poet's language' or 'pay close attention to the language of the poem'. Even when it does not state this directly, always comment on the poet's use of language in your answer. You could use REST to remember these features of poetic language:

**R**hythm and pace

**E**xpression

**S**ound effects

**T**one

When you comment on language, remember to use the correct technical terms when appropriate, such as:

❖ **alliteration** (repeated consonant sounds), e.g. 'blue-<u>d</u>ark <u>d</u>eer'

❖ **assonance** (repeated vowel sounds), e.g. '<u>ey</u>es meeting m<u>i</u>ne'

❖ **enjambment** (when a phrase runs over into the next line), e.g. 'in a brief/ split moment'

❖ **imagery** (the use of metaphor, simile or personification to draw a vivid picture), e.g. 'the curtain had blown aside for a moment'

❖ **onomatopoeia** (the sound of a word reflecting its meaning), e.g. 'came rustling across my path'.

Don't use these terms without commenting on their effect. Examiners call this 'feature spotting' and it will not get you any marks.

## Referring to the poems

When quotations are used well:

☑ they serve a purpose by illustrating a point

☑ the point is clearly explained

☑ they are not too long

☑ they are integrated into the candidate's own writing.

> **9** Read the extract from Student 1's essay below against the checklist above. Then read Student 2's work. Choose words from the poem extract provided above Student 2's work to complete the sentences.

### Student 1

*At the end, the creatures have become other-worldly, as they 'fly away up into the boil of big flakes', and the poet is left alone with his indelible memory of this brief but dramatic meeting.*

### Student 2

Then they ducked through the hedge, and upright they rode their legs
Away downhill over a snow-lonely field.

*The poet uses the expression '_____ _____' to describe how the deer move as if their legs are separate from their bodies. He shows his originality with language through the adjective '_____' to describe two aspects of the landscape in a single made-up word.*

# Developing your points on language

When you refer to a poem to make your point, don't leave it at that. Develop your point by making an additional comment showing how the quotation backs up your point. For example:

This is the main point that the student is making.

This is the evidence – quotes from the poem and reference to the poem.

The only stanza which **breaks the regular two line stanza pattern** and therefore stands out is stanza 7, which is just **the single line 'the deer had come for me'**. The **shock of this reflects the shock of the poet, and leaves the reader to wonder why they had come for him, or what their purpose was.**

This is a further comment which shows in detail how the evidence supports the main point.

**Remember** to 'flex your PECs' when commenting on language:

**P** – Point
**E** – Evidence
**C** – Comment

A good comment will improve your grade, because it shows (a) that you understand exactly how the poet has used language, and (b) that you are developing your interpretation of the poem.

10 These extracts from student essays all comment on the poet's language. They have been numbered in order of increasing effectiveness. Explain what makes each example better than the one before.

### Student 1

'Iguana Memory' has lots of childlike words: 'big like big big lizard with more legs than centipede so it seemed to me'. It also has some more interesting words like 'newleaf' and 'for the green of its life'.

### Student 3

'Iguana Memory' is an interesting mixture of simple vocabulary and images and intelligent wordplay. After the intriguing line 5, for example, which cleverly paints a picture of the sun picking out different colours on the ground, there is a very childlike passage. Repetition and simple words emphasise the size of the iguana, but in a way that shows the small size of the viewer as well.

### Student 2

'Iguana Memory' is an interesting mixture of simple vocabulary and images and intelligent wordplay. After the intriguing line 5, for example, where a made-up adjective ('newleaf') is used, there is the childlike 'big like big big lizard'.

### Student 4

'Iguana Memory' is an interesting mixture of simple vocabulary and images and intelligent wordplay. After the intriguing line 5, for example, where the made-up adjective 'newleaf' merges with the noun 'sunlight' to create a picture of the sun picking out different colours on the ground, there is the childlike 'big like big big lizard'. The repeated word emphasises the size, but in a way that shows the small size of the viewer as well.

11 Read the sample essay on pages 42–43.

(a) Identify two places where the student has developed the points about *Iguana Memory* by explaining the purpose of the quotation.

(b) The examiner wanted to see more precise focus on the language of *Roe-Deer*. Rewrite two of the student's points so that they comment in detail on the language used by the poet. Remember REST from page 40.

## 4 Work with student answers

You are now going to pull together all the learning you have done in this section by attempting a complete answer to a question on *Iguana Memory* and *Roe-Deer*. You will then study another student's answer for comparison.

> **12 (a)** First answer the question below. You have 40 minutes.
> **(b)** Then read the student answer and examiner comments below. Complete the activities in the boxes.

> Look again at *Iguana Memory* and *Roe-Deer*.
>
> How does each poem convey the nature and significance of these meetings?
>
> In your answer you should make close reference to the language of the poem.

**What makes this a good introduction?**

1   'Iguana Memory' by Grace Nichols and 'Roe-Deer' by Ted Hughes are both poems where animals and humans meet in a way which has significance. However, the two poems are different in tone and style, and the perspective which the two poets offer us of their meetings is also very different.

5   'Iguana Memory' appears a straightforward account of the young poet's first encounter with such a striking creature. Grace Nichols emphasises from the start that the encounter was significant to her partly because she was too young and inexperienced. This is achieved not only in the second line 'when I was a very small' (small, not young, to emphasise how childlike the experience is) but also

**Look at the first three paragraphs. Do you think the student has made a good start to the essay? Consider whether the student:**
- ☑ addresses the key words in the question
- ☑ comments on the poets' language right from the start

10   in the first line, which sounds like a child's casual conversation in tone 'saw an iguana once' (not 'I saw; and perhaps the word 'once' even has an echo of the opening word in all childhood fairytales). This impression of how young she was is kept going by childlike vocabulary – 'big like big big lizard' – using repetition just as a young child would. As well as its size, she describes the 'lizard' by

15   comparing it to other aspects of nature – 'green like morning newleaf sunlight'. The made-up word 'newleaf' is very effective, and just brings out how vivid and full of life the iguana was, to this young girl, as well as suggesting a particular shade of bright green, which young new leaves have. Also, the lack of capitals and punctuation throughout the poem tends to give it a childlike atmosphere.

20   Grace Nichols now begins to give this brief experience more significance. Because the creature was so new and thrilling to her it seems as though the iguana must be a new creation, something wonderful which has just entered the world. What is more, it is a two-way experience – 'eyes meeting mine/iguana and child looked in a brief split moment'. To put it simply, they are staring out

25   each other, she feels, in mutual amazement, before the iguana 'went hurrying/ for the green of its life', the pause between 'hurrying' and the final line cleverly suggesting the moment before it scurried off. Perhaps the writer wants us to

**Integrating quotations into your sentences is the best way of referring to the text. How has the student used quotations from the poems to explain and back up the points? Why do you think this works well?**

appreciate that, to the iguana, the little girl may have seemed 'big, big' and mysterious – or threatening, and presumably it did not encounter inquisitive

30   humans often. Grace Nichols' vocabulary also helps to bring the experience to life, as to make it clear to the reader why it was so memorable for her. As the iguana is a creature of the wild, she uses words from the world of nature to describe it – 'came rustling across my path', for example ( where 'path' seems a word from the human world); or 'more legs than a centipede', where the

35   hyperbole seems odd if you take it literally, but which describes very visibly how this new and exotic creature must have appeared to the surprised little girl.

40   Roe-Deer', on the other hand, is very different, in its tone and in its impact on the poet. On an otherwise deserted road 'in the dawn-dirty light', Ted Hughes encounters two deer who 'stared at me' before 'they rode their legs' to 'fly away up' out of his sight, leaving a strong impression. The significance for him seems to be how unusual and remarkable the sight was – he uses terms such as 'my snow-screen vision of the abnormal' which, after they have retreated in the woodland, sees life 'back to the ordinary'. The whole encounter was <u>extra</u> ordinary.

45   Perhaps he even suggests that the deer appeared for some supernatural or superstitious reason, when he writes 'they had happened into my dimension/the moment I was arriving just there'. He certainly feels that the deer are playing just as active a part in the encounter as he is (perhaps like Grace Nichols' iguana staring at her) when he writes 'I could think the deer were waiting for me/To remember the password or sign'. This is strengthened by the fact that the only

50   stanza which breaks the regular two line stanza pattern and therefore stands out is stanza 7, which is just the single line 'the deer had come for me'. The shock of this reflects the shock of the poet, and leaves the reader to wonder why they had come for him, or what their purpose was. Perhaps they were protecting their world (the 'password') from the unwelcome intrusion of the humans: certainly there is a strong

55   feeling that there is some kind of communication (or maybe a failure, or a missed opportunity, to communicate) between the humans and the creatures.

  The language used to describe the encounter also plays its part in bringing this strange meeting to life, and giving it significance. The two hyphenated expressions 'dawn-dirty' and 'blue-dark deer' are strongly alliterative to emphasise the

60   importance of the encounter. In fact the atmosphere of this encounter is probably what stays impressed in the reader's mind – when the deer 'rode their legs' (an odd but striking metaphor) to the 'snow-lonely' (another effective hyphenated expression) field, and then he watched them 'fly away'. At the end, the creatures have become other-worldly, as they 'fly away up into the boil of big flakes', and the

65   poet is left alone with his indelible memory of this brief but dramatic meeting.

  This is obviously on a different scale and in a different tone from Grace Nichols' childish fascination with the strange iguana. Yet the poems are similar, in that in each case an animal/human encounter is brought to life vividly and effectively by the poet's use of language, and in each case we are able to appreciate and share

70   the significance of the moments.

---

The student has planned the answer by poem rather than by theme. How has this plan been made clear to the reader? Look at the first sentence of each paragraph. This will often tell you what the paragraph is about.

How well has the student shown an understanding of how Ted Hughes uses language and poetic devices to create effects? Identify one place where it has been done well, and one where this could be improved, giving your reasons.

Add a comment to explain how the quotation 'fly away up into the boil of big flakes' helps to make the point.

How well has the student concluded the essay? Does the ending refer to any of the key words in the question? Does it sum up the student's view?

## The examiner's view

A very good answer. The focus on the question is strong throughout, and the balance between the poems is good; they are also linked neatly at times. There is a thorough understanding of both poems and the student's ideas are expressed fluently, with some perceptive comments at times. To improve the answer's grade to an A*, the student could have developed the comments on language further, especially on *Roe-Deer*.

**A grade A answer**

13   Assess your own answer against this A grade answer. Look at the 'Steps to success in reading' on page 7 to check how well you are meeting the assessment objectives. What do you need to work on to improve your grade?

**Remember** that you cannot practise too much. Areas such as planning, writing good openings and ensuring that you comment on the poets' use of language will improve very quickly when you practise.

Now is the time to put everything in this unit into practice for yourself.

**14** Allow 40 minutes, and choose one of the questions below.

When you have finished, assess yourself against your answer to the question in Activity 12, or swap your work with your partner and assess each other's. Look back at the 'Steps to success in reading' on page 7 to identify exactly where you are doing well and where you need to improve. Note down three areas in which you would like to improve, and practise those skills.

**Remember** to begin by thinking about the focus of the question. What are the key words? Then spend no more than a few minutes planning your answer.

**1** Look again at *The Horses* and ONE other poem from **Nature** in which the poet looks at the experience of being old.

How do the natural images help the poets express their ideas?

In your answer you should make close reference to the language of the poems.

*(Higher Tier)*

**2** Look again at *Keeping Orchids* and *Nettles*.

How do the poets use the image of flowers to make their point?

For each poem you should comment on:

❖ what the flowers mean for the person in the poem
❖ how the details of the flowers relate to the points being made
❖ the way the poets use language.

*(Foundation Tier)*

**3** Look again at *The Stag* and ONE other poem from **Nature** which describes an animal or fish. Discuss the ways in which the poets paint a picture of the animal.

For each poem you should comment on:

❖ the attitude of the poet to the animal

❖ how the language of the poem is used to paint the picture

❖ any similarities or differences between the poems.

*(Foundation Tier)*

**4** Look again at *Wind* and *The Storm*. Compare the poets' description of a storm, and the methods they use to describe it.

In your answer you should make close reference to the language of the poems.

*(Higher Tier)*

# B Reading non-fiction prose

By the end of this section you will have sharpened three skills that will help you to improve your answer on non-fiction prose:

1 comment on a non-fiction text, don't just describe it

2 comment on the writer's choice and use of language

3 recognise how writers of non-fiction use fact and opinion.

You will then explore the qualities of answers at different grades and assess your skills through writing an answer to a non-fiction prose question, similar to the one you will meet in the exam.

## Non-fiction prose

The non-fiction you are studying in the Anthology divides into two types:

◆ **Literary non-fiction** such as travel writing and autobiography, in which the writers describe real-life experiences. Their purposes include to inform, to entertain and to reflect on experience.

◆ **Newspaper articles** that focus on the themes of 'Sport for All' and 'Parents and Children'. They contain individual opinions and ideas and often some personal experience. Their main purposes are to argue and inform.

## What is the examiner looking for?

1 Below are the characteristics of a good answer and of a weak answer. Find the pairs of comments that match. This activity will focus your attention on the qualities that will gain you marks in this section of the exam. The first pair has been done for you.

| A good answer | A weak answer |
| --- | --- |
| • stays focused on what the question is asking | • refers to the question once then goes off in another direction |

A summarises the content without commenting on tone, form or audience

E stays focused on what the question is asking

I comments on what is happening in the text

B refers to the question once then goes off in another direction

J focuses on naming the techniques that the writer uses

G supports the points made by referring often to the text

D shows awareness of the form of the text (e.g. article, diary, autobiography) the intended audience and the tone (e.g. amusing, frightening, angry)

C sums up the writer's arguments without comment on technique

F describes what is happening in the text

H quotes from the text at great length

IN THE EXAM
SPECIFICATION A

■ There is one question. It will be based on one named extract or article from the non-fiction prose section of The Edexcel Anthology.

■ The question usually asks you to 'discuss' or 'comment' on key aspects of the text.

■ This question is worth 10% of your total mark for GCSE English.

■ You must answer the question in 40 minutes.

■ Your answer to this question will be assessed against Reading assessment objectives (i) and (v). See page 6.

When assessing your reading skills, the examiner will be seeing how well you can:

❖ show your understanding of the text

❖ develop your points.

You need to do both of these things to improve your grade.

## Understand the audience and purpose

To comment effectively on a non-fiction text, it helps to understand who it is being written for (the audience) and why it is being written (the purpose or aim).

**2** Think about the audience and purpose of each of the non-fiction texts in the Anthology. You can make an informed guess about intended audience by looking at the topic and the sort of language used. Copy and complete the grid below, taking answers from the list underneath the grid.

(Note: a text may have more than one purpose and audience. You will be adding information and a column to this grid as the section progresses, so give yourself plenty of space, and set it out in landscape format.)

| Text | Form | Purpose/aim | Audience | |
|---|---|---|---|---|
| *Mongolian Wedding* | | | | |
| *The Other Side of the Dale* | | to narrate<br>to entertain | | |
| *The Lady in the Van* | | | | |
| *Don't leave me here to die* | | | well-educated general readers<br>those with an interest in travel | |
| 'Save our children from the horrors of school sport' | Newspaper article | | | |
| 'School sports culture leads to violence' | | to inform<br>to argue | | |

*Forms:* travel writing, autobiography, diary entries, newspaper articles

*Purpose/aim:* to persuade, to describe, to advise, to explain, to instruct, to entertain, to narrate, to analyse, to review, to inform, to argue, to reflect

*Audiences:* teenagers, middle-aged readers, well-educated general readers, parents, those with an interest in education, those with an interest in sport, those with an interest in family issues, those with an interest in travel

# Show your understanding

Weak answers spend a lot of time describing what happens in a text. Simply describing does not show your understanding. To show your understanding, you need to focus more on commenting on the text.

Commenting means saying something interesting about the text that relates to the question. Comments could include:

❖ your own ideas or feelings about the text (make sure that these are directly related to the text and not just general personal comments on the subject or anecdotal opinions)

❖ examples from the text that back up your points in detail

❖ explaining how the writer uses language for a particular effect (e.g. below, Student 2 explains how the writer creates a contrast between the newly-married couple and the wedding guests)

❖ points about the organisation of the text (e.g. a comment about how a text begins or ends, whether the text is organised in a chronological sequence of events, or how the argument develops)

❖ points about the background or context that influences what the author writes (e.g. much of the humour in *Mongolian Wedding* comes from comparisons with our own experiences of weddings).

3 Two students are commenting on the humour in *Mongolian Wedding*. Read the extracts from their essays below and answer the questions.

## Student 1

Stewart uses a funny style to make us laugh. He describes how the bride's elder sister falls off the back of the truck when she arrives at the wedding. The bride was very round and the bridegroom was long and thin. The old ladies at the wedding were disapproving and spent the whole time kneeing him in the back. The more drunk they get, the louder everyone gets until everyone ends up singing a song. Of course they end up fighting!

How much of this answer is description rather than comment?

Does the answer show that the student has analysed the text?

## Student 2

The narrator's humorous style engages the reader and the text is rich with entertaining examples, such as the same tradition that demands the bride hides from her groom also ironically reveals her hiding place! Stewart invites us to laugh at the drunken family members who get off the truck, but his description is polite and respectful, using the euphemism 'dishevelled merriment'. The scene is extremely comic. The bizarre tug of war that results from the bride's family's attempts to leave early contrast with the static and passive nature of the bridal couple who, amidst the chaos, 'sat side by side'.

How much of this answer is description rather than comment?

Identify two comments on the text that the student makes.

Based on what you have read so far, is this answer stronger than Student 1's?

**4** This extract is from an essay about the effect of language in the article 'Pay your children too much attention' (p 65). It contains too much description and not enough evidence. Improve it by finding a quotation from the article to support the highlighted statement.

> *'Pay your children too much attention' is a very reasonable article. The writer begins by describing what 'an expert' has said about the dangerous way parents 'hothouse' their children. This expert is then revealed to be Matthew Melmed, chief executive of Zero to Three. He refers to research that the organisation has carried out to prove that children can be overstimulated. All this is very reasonable, and* ==the language of the article is reasonable== *too, though it gets more emotive at the end.*

*Is there any evidence to support this point?*

## Develop your points

When you make a point or a comment, develop it by:
❖ going into more detail
❖ referring to another example of the same feature/technique
❖ making a link with something else you have said in your essay
❖ in fact, anything to show a deeper understanding of the text.

**5** Read the two paragraphs from a student's answer to the question: 'How does the writer of 'Use persuasion not Coercion' present her views'? Answer the questions in the boxes.

*Find an example of 'forthright' language in the first paragraph of the article.*

> *In this* ==forthright== *and plain-speaking article, Bunting's aim and audience are two-fold. She is discussing the issue of whether it is right for parents to smack their children, so partly she is addressing those parents who use physical force.*
>
> *But the author directs most of her anger and personal views towards those people who actually make the laws, to dissuade the law-makers from introducing what she feels is a 'ludicrous intervention' – a ban on smacking children under three. She criticises the 'Scottish executives' for their proposal, and in some places she directly addresses the law-makers: 'By all means campaign against parents...run parenting classes...'. Her three main points are that you have to persuade, not force, parents to change their behaviour (note the title of the article, which is directed at the lawmakers); that the law cannot be enforced; and that laws are to punish crimes, whereas violent parents need help.*

*Explain how the final sentence develops the points made earlier in the second paragraph.*

**6 (a)** Use your commenting skills to write a paragraph on the question below.

**Remember** to:
• make comments on the text rather than describing it
• develop the points that you make.

**(b)** Swap your work with a partner. Mark where they have used a simple description (put 'descr' in the margin), made a comment (write 'comm' in the margin), or developed a point (give them a tick).

> What do we learn about Miss S. from the way Alan Bennett describes the social worker's visit (*The Lady in the Van*, p.56)?

# 2 Comment on the writer's choice and use of language

A good answer will examine the language of an extract, not just describe what happens in it. Examiners will expect you to use the correct language terminology when analysing these texts.

You are now going to identify the different types of language that non-fiction texts use. You will then practise commenting on the language.

## The language of literary non-fiction

The first four pieces in the Anthology (pp.47–59) are examples of literary non-fiction. Their main purpose is to narrate events in an entertaining and compelling way.

Writers of literary non-fiction often use descriptive language to engage their readers' attention. Some of the key features of descriptive language are:

1 **Going into detail** – particular events, people, places, objects, etc. are described in detail. This takes the reader into the writer's world.

2 **Powerful words** – strong, interesting nouns, verbs, adjectives and adverbs all add colour and power to a narrative.

3 **Techniques** such as repetition, contrast and varied sentence length also add power.

4 **Imagery** – writers describe something by linking it to something else. The two main techniques are the simile (e.g. 'His legs were *like* lead weights') and the metaphor (e.g. 'His legs *were* lead weights').

5 **Using the senses** – the reader hears, sees, smells, feels and tastes the scene.

**EXAM TIP**

You will gain marks in the non-fiction prose question by commenting on *what* the writers say and *how* they say it. No marks are given for commenting on the way the non-fiction piece is visually laid out on the page, so don't waste time writing about what it 'looks like'.

> 7 Match up the Anthology extracts below with the features of descriptive language listed above.

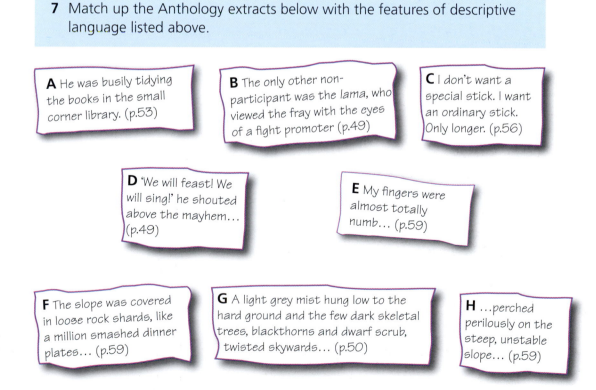

**A** He was busily tidying the books in the small corner library. (p.53)

**B** The only other non-participant was the lama, who viewed the fray with the eyes of a fight promoter (p.49)

**C** I don't want a special stick. I want an ordinary stick. Only longer. (p.56)

**D** 'We will feast! We will sing!' he shouted above the mayhem… (p.49)

**E** My fingers were almost totally numb… (p.59)

**F** The slope was covered in loose rock shards, like a million smashed dinner plates… (p.59)

**G** A light grey mist hung low to the hard ground and the few dark skeletal trees, blackthorns and dwarf scrub, twisted skywards… (p.50)

**H** …perched perilously on the steep, unstable slope… (p.59)

**8** Add a new column to the grid you started on page 46, with the heading 'language features'. List at least four examples of descriptive language in each Anthology piece as shown below.

| Text | Form | Purpose/aim | Audience | Language features |
|---|---|---|---|---|
| *Mongolian Wedding* | | | | *Detail*, e.g. the description of breakfast<br><br>*Powerful words*, e.g. 'dishevelled merriment'<br><br>*Imagery*, e.g. 'he chopped two sisters to the ground'<br><br>*Senses*, e.g. 'the sharp knees in his back' |

> *Remember* to flex your PECs:
> - Point – make a point about the language used
> - Evidence – quote briefly from the text, or refer to the text
> - Comment – make a comment on how the language creates its effect.

# Comment on language of literary non-fiction

To get a good grade you need to do more than list the language features or techniques that a writer uses. You must also comment on the language.

Commenting on language means:

- ☑ analysing the effect a writer's language has on the reader
- ☑ referring closely to the text.

Two students are discussing the military imagery used in *Mongolian Wedding*. Military imagery means words and phrases associated with battle. Notice their different approaches:

**Grade C student**

> Far too vague with no textual evidence. No discussion of the effect of the imagery.

> Stanley Stewart uses lots of battle words to describe the bride and groom's big day. There is a lot of arguing going on and no one really seems happy.

**Grade A student**

> Good comment on the effect of the imagery. Relevant evidence from the text given.

> Military terminology occurs frequently, emphasising the war-like and troubled relationship between these two families: 'look-outs...camp... armies...ranks...victory.' This is clearly not going to be an easy union for the 'happy' couple!

**9** Read the extract below from 'Don't leave me here' and the three responses. The students are discussing the writer's use of language in the extract.

Match up each response opposite with the correct examiner's comment.

> We stood to throw away an entire expedition: the money, the time, the thousands of vertical feet of physical and mental effort. We had sponsors who expected us to go for the summit. We had personal ambitions that pointed in the same direction. We were only 240 vertical metres from the top, only four or five hours in climbing time. We were so close to fulfilling everything we had set out to do.

## Student 1

'We' is repeated five times at the start of a sentence, which shows the writer is making an effect, she is emphasising it was so important to actually get to the top and the repeated word shows how it all depended on her efforts (and the group, as it is 'we' not 'I'). There is a metaphor in the first sentence too, which is powerful.

## Student 2

There is lots of repetition in this paragraph, such as 'we' and 'only'. Cathy O'Dowd feels like she does not want to turn back because if she does that then she will lose a lot of things. Also, it would be a complete waste of time and money – and it's not her paying for it as she tells us that she has sponsors.

## Student 3

Repetition is a common feature of the text. The use of the first person plural is repeated five times at the start of a sentence, reinforcing the strength O'Dowd feels as part of a group which of course contrasts sharply with the isolation of the dying woman. By using a pattern of three in the first sentence, we are made to focus on the incredible amount of loss that would result if their attempt at conquering Everest were to be abandoned. It is very much a case of 'so near, yet so far' which is reflected in the repetition of 'only' close to the end of this paragraph.

### Examiner's comment a)

This response gives a good comment on the effect of repetition, and ties it in to the text, although the explanation could be expressed more clearly. It also provides evidence by making relevant reference to the text. But it simply names one other language feature without giving evidence or comment.

### Examiner's comment b)

This response is excellent. It recognises a range of the language features in the extract, and gives the correct terminology. It links the point being made by referring closely to the text. Above all, it explains in detail what effect these techniques have on a reader.

### Examiner's comment c)

This response mentions only one language feature and gives two examples. But it makes no attempt to discuss what effect that feature has – why it might have been used. The comments do not relate clearly enough to the language choice of the writer.

10  (a)  Look carefully at the first 56 lines of *The Other Side of the Dale*. Write one paragraph on how Gervase Phinn uses language to set the scene. Cover the place and the people in your answer.

Remember to:
- back up your points with short quotations or references to the text
- comment on the effect of the writer's language.

Here is one point to get you started… *The school inspector's arrival unsettles the teacher, Mrs Durdon. She 'smiled weakly', her hand 'trembled slightly' and she 'blinked rapidly'. The adverbs 'weakly', 'slightly' and 'rapidly' effectively express the nervousness which she cannot hide.*

(b)  Now swap with a friend and ask him/her to add one or two constructive comments on how you could gain more marks. Rewrite the paragraph in the light of these comments.

### EXAM TIP

Don't simply list technical terms such as 'metaphor', 'list of three' and expect the examiner to be impressed. The examiner will only give you marks if you make a comment on them, by saying how they create the effect that the writer wants.

**Remember** that the precise language and approach that the writer uses depends on their purpose. So it is important to be clear about the purpose of each of the articles before you comment on it.

# The language of newspaper articles

The remaining eight pieces in the non-fiction section of the Anthology (pp.47–59) are newspaper articles. These articles have one or both of these main purposes:

❖ to **argue** about an issue so well that the reader agrees with the writer's point of view. They have a personal view which is sustained through the article.

❖ to **inform** readers about an issue. The emphasis is on facts and on describing the arguments of other people.

> **11** Look back in the grid you compiled on page 46.
>
> **(a)** Check that your 'Text' and 'Purpose/aim' comments on the 'Sport for All?' articles look something like this:
>
> | Text | Purpose/aim |
> | --- | --- |
> | Save our children from the horrors of school sport | to argue |
> | School sports culture leads to violence | to argue (also to inform) |
> | Mind games | to inform (also to argue) |
> | Sport in schools | to argue |
>
> **(b)** Look at the 'Parents and Children' articles again. Make sure that the 'Purpose' column accurately describes the balance of argument and information in each text. Only one article aims mainly to argue for the personal views of the writer – which one?

### A TO A*

To ensure that you get as many marks as possible, make it crystal clear in your answer who is actually doing the arguing in the text. Many of the newspaper articles are mainly information texts in which the arguments are not the views of the writer. The writer is referring to or quoting other people's views. When referring to 'Pay your children' (p.65), for example, say 'The writer quotes Elizabeth Howell, who uses emotive words …' rather than 'The writer uses emotive words …'.

Texts which argue often contain these features:

**1 powerful and emotive language** (emotive language is designed to make the reader feel something strongly)

**2 logical language**, often using signpost words and phrases to emphasise how one thing follows from another (e.g. 'therefore', 'by contrast')

**3 rhetorical techniques**, such as repetition, lists of three, rhetorical questions (Are we afraid?), directly addressing the reader

**4 opinions** rather than facts (an opinion is someone's view that cannot be proved to be true, while a fact can be checked and found to be true or untrue).

> **12** Match each of the short extracts below to the language features listed above.

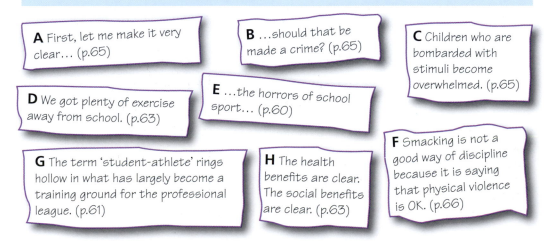

A First, let me make it very clear… (p.65)

B …should that be made a crime? (p.65)

C Children who are bombarded with stimuli become overwhelmed. (p.65)

D We got plenty of exercise away from school. (p.63)

E …the horrors of school sport… (p.60)

F Smacking is not a good way of discipline because it is saying that physical violence is OK. (p.66)

G The term 'student-athlete' rings hollow in what has largely become a training ground for the professional league. (p.61)

H The health benefits are clear. The social benefits are clear. (p.63)

Newspaper articles which inform often contain these language features:

❖ plain, precise sentences to convey the information clearly
❖ formal language and a reasonable tone to help readers feel they can trust the information given
❖ facts and specific details given to support the conclusion being drawn
❖ other people's views quoted to give a range of perspectives.

**13** Read 'Mind games' (p.62) again. Try to find two examples of each of the language features listed above.

**14** Collect examples of all of the language features used in the newspaper articles and add them to the third column in the grid you started on page 50.

## Comment on language of newspaper articles

Now that you have identified some of the language features used in the articles, you need to be able to comment on their effect. There are no marks for simply spotting the features and listing them!

Commenting on language means:
❖ analysing the effect a writer's language has on the reader
❖ referring closely to the text
❖ linking this in with the purpose of the writer.

You must comment on the language of the newspaper articles to get a higher grade. The method you should use is the same as for literary non-fiction (page 50). With newspaper articles, however, when you comment on the purpose of the writer it is important to bear in mind whether their aim is mainly to argue or to inform.

**15** Read the extracts from students' responses below. The students are discussing how the writers use language to achieve their aims. Read the examiner comments and answer the questions.

**Student 1**

Wendy Berliner in 'Mind games' organises her sentences into long paragraphs. The paragraphs are all very long, there isn't a single short one. This shows that she isn't going for any dramatic effects, and that everything is balanced well, as it should be because she is trying to give full coverage of the view that PE makes you cleverer.

The first part of this paragraph is good: the student describes the language feature (long paragraphs), gives evidence, and comments on why the writer chose to write this way. Find one paragraph you could refer to in order to support the point made here.

**Student 2**

Duncan McNeill gives his own opinions throughout 'Sport in schools'. He often refers to his own experience too. The whole article has a personal feel – this seems to be his truly felt view.

The student makes a good point, but it lacks support. Continue the paragraph to include some evidence from the article – this could push the student up a grade.

**Student 3**

Duncan McNeill uses humour to get his argument across in 'Sport in schools'. This is a very effective and persuasive technique.

The student makes an important point, but doesn't develop it. Rewrite the paragraph so that it refers closely to the text and comments on the effect of the language. This could push the student up a grade.

## 3 Recognise how fact and opinion are used

*Remember*, a fact is something that can be proved true, e.g. 'The school week was lengthened by 9.5 hours'. You could find out if this is true by checking a reliable source.

One special feature of newspaper articles that you need to understand is their use of facts and opinions.

Facts can be presented in different ways:

☑ **as statements of things that are the case**, or that have occurred, e.g. 'Mr Biddulph has taught discipline skills to more than 3,000 parents in countries from Spain to China' (p.64)

☑ **as references to statistics or surveys**, e.g. 'According to a survey … only 11 per cent of children aged six to eight spent two hours or more a week in PE lessons last year' (p.60)

☑ **as examples from the writer's or others' experience**, e.g. 'We lived in the bottom flat with our TV aerial in the tenement loft' (p.63).

**16** Find three more facts in the newspaper articles. (Note: you are more likely to find facts in the articles that aim to inform as well as to argue; see page 52 above.)

Facts lend authority to a text, but the way they are used can be questioned too. If you want to improve your grade, you must be able to evaluate how facts help the writer, and question their real effectiveness.

**17** Read the grid below. Draw up a similar grid to evaluate how effectively your three extra facts, from Activity 15, are used.

## EXAM TIP

To get a good grade, you need to be able to spot the different ways in which opinions influence the reader. This means paying close attention to the language used by the writer.

| Fact | How it adds authority to the text | How effective is it? |
|---|---|---|
| Mr Biddulph has taught discipline skills to more than 3,000 parents in countries from Spain to China | He is an expert with lots of experience | 'from Spain to China' suggests internationally known, but is 3,000 that many? |
| …we got plenty of exercise away from school, chasing buses, sugar lorries, ice cream vans and milk motors' | Personal experience backs up the argument | The humour gets the point over well, but is perhaps exaggerated |

*Remember*, an opinion is just someone's point of view that cannot be proved true, e.g. 'School sport and PE have been squeezed and neglected in recent years'. This is the writer's opinion – would your opinion be different?

Opinions are often presented in ways that give a very one-sided view:

❖ by adding powerful adjectives, adverbs, nouns or verbs, e.g. 'the <u>relentless rise</u> of college sports has taken its toll', '

❖ by using words with a positive or negative slant (connotation), e.g. 'a parade of concerned sporting figures <u>waffled on</u> about the necessity of 'instilling' sport in kids from a young age'

❖ by adding phrases to deceive the readers into accepting the opinion as fact or get them on the writer's side, e.g. 'All parents know…', 'In fact …'.

**18** Read the following paragraph from 'Save our children…' and the extracts from two student essays which comment on the way the writer puts forward his views. Which of the two responses best analyses the effect of the writer's language?

> In fact, the tradition of making sport synonymous with such treats as public embarrassment and being forced to act against one's will tended to put off even the people who were good at it.

**Student 1**

Is John Harris expressing a fact or an opinion? Is it a fact that those who were good at sport were put off it at school? The writer's craft here is to dress up opinion as fact by making it seem as though what he is writing is the truth. He does this primarily by starting his point of view 'In fact' which is designed to trick us and manipulate us into thinking what he goes on to say is a fact.

**Student 2**

John Harris is a skilful manipulator of words who makes his opinions look like facts. His opinion is that school sport used to be an 'embarrassment' (note the emotive term, which evokes the picture of being the last to be chosen for the team) and put off even the good sportspeople. The opinion is actually not very well backed up – no real evidence is given, and he uses the word 'tended' to show that this didn't always happen. But his clever language and the way he begins with 'in fact' actually makes the opinion very persuasive.

Look carefully at the heading on page 61 of the Anthology: 'School sports culture leads to violence'.

Here are two student responses to this heading.

**Student 1**

In the headline the writer explains the fact that school sport in America has resulted in violence. He is a persuasive writer since he goes on to explain exactly what he means by this, for example, that if you are not good at sport you get bullied by those who are good at it. Because he mentions a newspaper in America, 'the Los Angeles Times', we know he is telling the truth.

**Student 2**

This controversial headline concerning student athletes in America deliberately provokes our response as it is a shocking statement – and a good example of opinion masquerading as fact. If we read this one headline alone, we would go away thinking that sport in schools has led to violence everywhere and at all times ('leads' is ambiguous here). Obviously this is not the case since it is Julian Borger's opinion and we need to read the article to discover the extent of the truth, if at all, of this headline.

**19** The examiner's notes on the above responses are muddled up on the next page. Sort them out into two groups by compiling a table like the one below.

| Points about Student 1's response | Points about Student 2's response |
|---|---|
| • | • |

- The student thinks that a confident statement is a proven fact. There is no awareness that the writer might be using a persuasive technique here.

- The student keeps an open mind, remains objective and looks for evidence that will support the assertions being made.

- The student needs to develop the point that he is a persuasive writer, and explain how he is persuasive, that is, the methods he uses.

- The idea that because something appeared in a newspaper makes it true is not of course correct. Reference to other newspapers can, however, add authority to an article.

- The student recognises that headlines can be deliberately crafted to look like fact.

- The student develops the point, makes reference to the text and recognises that careful choice of words can dress up opinions as facts.

20 Now put all your skills in recognising and evaluating facts and opinions into practice.

   (a) Write three paragraphs on the exam question below. Remember to:
   - pay attention to both facts and opinions, and evaluate their effect
   - comment on how the writer's language gives the opinions impact
   - back up your points with short quotations or references to the text.

   Here is an idea to get you started: 'The writer often uses humour to make the opinions expressed more convincing by winning over the reader. For example, …'

   (b) Now swap with a friend and ask them to add two or three constructive comments on how you could gain more marks. Rewrite your answer in the light of their comments.

What persuasive techniques does 'Save our children' on page 60 of the Anthology use to influence you? Refer to the writer's use of facts and opinions in your answer.

You are now going to pull together all the learning you have done in this section by attempting a complete answer. You will then study two other students' answers for comparison. You will also remind yourself of some effective ways of planning and structuring your answer, so that you can boost its grade.

**21 (a)** First answer the question below. You have 40 minutes.

**(b)** Then read the students' answers and examiner comments below. Answer the questions in the boxes.

> Look again in The Edexcel Anthology at Alan Bennett's description of *The Lady in the Van* (pp.55–57).
>
> How does Alan Bennett portray Miss S.'s personality and chosen lifestyle?
>
> Give evidence from the text to support your views.

**Student 1**

1  Alan Bennett shows Miss S. as quite different from a lot of women. Most women do not live in a caravan in someone's front garden like she does. She's a bit like a tramp really, or a bag lady, but the real difference is that she does have a home to go to so doesn't have to sleep on the streets.
5  Her windows are dirty as Alan Bennett tells us the caravan has a 'murky windscreen' so this tells me she doesn't clean it very often and inside her van she has got old clothes, lots of bags and food that is half finished. So she's a bit dirty really.

Miss S. is a bit moody too as she doesn't really want to speak to anyone.
10  She is also religious as she bends over to pray. It's funny that she told Vincent Price to shut up as he is the actor with the scary voice and talked on Michael Jackson's Thriller song – but maybe she didn't know it was him as it was dark! When Miss S. is making petrol herself she sounds a bit like a witch mixing a spell as she uses 'a spoonful' and 'a pinch'. I can just
15  imagine her looking like a witch actually with her messy hair and clothes. And it must mean she is tight and not got much money if she's trying to make her own petrol because petrol does cost a lot I think. Her clothes seem really wacky as she wears lots of weird hats and a scarf and big skirts and most of them were brightly coloured. One time she got picked
20  up by the police because they thought her dress was a nightie, so she's not that careful what she wears. But she's also rude to the policeman when all he is trying to do is help her. I think she is quite stubborn as well and likes to do what she wants, not what other people want her to do.

*Sidebar comments:*

This answer launches straight into detail. Compare Student 2's first paragraph. Which is a better introduction, and why?

The point about the dirt inside the van could be improved by commenting on the language used. Add a comment on Bennett's phrase 'a midden of old clothes, plastic bags and half-eaten foods'.

The student makes lots of points here, but they are mostly descriptive and not all are supported or developed. This is how the first point could be developed:

*If she hears any movement at night 'she would straightaway switch off the light and wait, like an animal that has been disturbed ...'*

Write a comment about the underlined simile and what it tells us about Miss S.

25 Miss S. seems to be a proud lady as well because she didn't like it when she thought other people might think it's her that stinks of manure. And another reason she's rude is because the social worker was only trying to help but she was horrible to her as she says 'I only asked for one coat'. She's ungrateful I think. Alan Bennett uses a simile to describe her 'like a chimpanzee'.

30 It's funny that she says 'frisbee' when she means 'freebie' though, that makes us laugh that she gets that word wrong. I think she's also a private person because she doesn't normally tell the man about her life.

At the end Alan Bennett tells us again about how dirty her lifestyle is because 'she stands there in her grimy raincoat, strands of lank grey hair
35 escaping from under her headscarf'. I don't know why he does but he does seem to feel sorry for her as he's glad that the other people on the day trip have been nice to her that day.

Overall I think Miss S. likes to keep herself to herself and doesn't like mixing with other people.

## The examiner's view

This candidate shows a sound understanding of Miss S. and makes a good range of relevant points. Some of the ideas are developed better than others but there is a definite awareness of how Bennett presents Miss S. The student could improve the answer by developing the points further and attending to the structure of the essay (paragraphing, and including an effective introduction and conclusion).

**A grade C answer**

22 Assess your own answer against this C grade answer. Look at the 'Steps to success in reading' on page 7 to check how well you are meeting the assessment objectives. What do you need to work on to improve your grade?

**Student 2**

1　Alan Bennett presents Miss S. as being a very eccentric, opinionated and determined character. He describes in detail her unusual character, her long stay in Bennett's front garden and her strange lifestyle.

5　Bennett uses a matter of fact style when describing Miss S., which makes it sound like what she was doing was normal. An example of this is, 'perhaps by now inevitably, the van and Miss S. ended up in my garden'. Another is 'I had run a cable out from the house to give her light and heating'. This creates humour because she is an uninvited guest and he is looking after her needs. The reader expects him to react very differently to the situation
10　and character and to complain. Bennett also uses similes in a humorous way; for example: 'like Excalibur' is a deliberately exaggerated image.

Bennett does not really judge Miss S. for her appearance and lifestyle and leaves the reader to do that. This also adds humour because Bennett does not really care that Miss S. is living in his front garden – an unusual
15　reaction. Humour is used to present the character of Miss S. and her lifestyle because it is so ridiculous that it is funny. An example of this is shown when Miss S. makes some homemade petrol, using a recipe for 'petrol substitute' which she had read about in a paper. She was quite surprised when the van failed to work using her homemade petrol.

20　Miss S. is presented as rather rude and ungrateful, as when she is brought new coats by her social worker she says 'I only asked for one': she does not want to be pitied or thought of as a charity case. She also appears very rude when two film stars, one being Vincent Price, went to see Bennett and she told them to 'pipe down' because she was 'trying to sleep'. This again
25　creates humour because of the ludicrous nature of the situation. She has parked her van, uninvited, on his garden and she has the audacity to tell callers to be quiet.

Miss S. is presented as being unsociable, as when she heard any movement she would 'switch off the light and wait', since she did not want to see
30　anyone. She is likened to an animal in several places through this extract – for example, 'turning over the contents of the box like a chimpanzee', but Bennett never judges her.

Bennett uses euphemisms when describing Miss S.'s appearance, such as 'sturdy slippered leg', which shows Bennett does not dislike Miss S. Her
35　clothing is described using colourful language, and even though it is made of rags, Bennett tries to see something good in them – for example, 'Her skirts had a telescopic appearance' and 'one skirt was made by sewing several orange dusters together'. Hats were also always a feature.

Notice how this student shows a strong grasp of the question by referring to the key words (portray, personality, lifestyle) throughout this answer. Often synonyms are used for variety (e.g. presents, character). Identify six places in the essay where the key words or their synonyms are used.

The student's use of paragraphs and careful organisation show that the answer has been carefully planned.

This essay gains lots of marks by commenting on the text rather than describing it. Comment shows understanding. Identify which bits of paragraphs 2 and 3 are description and which are comment.

How could the student improve the answer by developing the point about Miss S.'s hats? Read lines 50–54 of the text again and comment on the effect of Bennett's description.

Here the student makes a point, gives some evidence and makes a further comment. Find two other places in the essay where this effective way of writing is used.

The highlighted point is a bit vague. How could this student improve the answer by showing how the writer uses language to create sympathy?

40 Miss S. is presented as having some pride in herself and she cares what other people think of her. This is shown when Bennett gets manure delivered and Miss S. is 'concerned that people passing might think the smell' is coming from her. Bennett portrays her character by showing her independence and the way she tries to make the best of what she has.

45 Because of the skill of Bennett's writing, the reader has some sympathy for Miss S. as when she goes on her 'freebie', which she mistakenly calls her 'Frisbee', she is really happy and reacts in a normal manner.

The examples from the text indicate that Miss S. is certainly presented in highly colourful language. Bennett does not judge her. He leaves the reader to draw their own conclusions. However, the sympathetic way in which he gives a picture of her life and character makes this an interesting portrait,
50 despite the unconventional style of her life.

## The examiner's view

The essay explores Bennett's portrait of Miss S. in depth, looking particularly closely at the humour of his description and comment. The response shows a good understanding of the text and makes a range of well-observed points, some of which are developed substantially. The analysis is thoughtful and there is a good use of examples from the text.

**A grade A answer**

> **23** Assess your own answer against this A grade answer. Look at the 'Steps to success in reading' on page 7 to check how well you are meeting the assessment objectives. What do you need to work on to improve your grade?

# 5 Exam question practice

Now is the time to put everything in this section into practice for yourself.

**24** Allow 40 minutes, and choose one of the questions below.

When you have finished, assess yourself against your answer to the question in Activity 21, or swap your work with a partner and assess each other's. Look back at the 'Steps to success in reading' on page 7 to identify where you are doing well and where you need to improve. Note down three areas in which you would like to improve, and practise those skills.

**Remember** that you cannot practise too much. Areas such as planning, writing good openings and ensuring that you comment on the poet's use of language will improve very quickly when you practise.

**1** Look again in The Edexcel Anthology at the article 'Smacking not the answer, say kids'.

What different points of view about smacking do the young people express in the article?

You should consider what these young people think about:

❖ the effect of smacking on children's relationships with their parents
❖ how parents should act
❖ what is wrong with relying on physical punishment.

Support your answer with examples from the text.

*(Foundation Tier)*

**2** Look again in The Edexcel Anthology at the article 'Parents learn how to say NO'.

What does this article reveal about attitudes to bringing up children and the importance of discipline?

Give evidence from the text to support your views. *(Higher Tier)*

**3** Look again in The Edexcel Anthology at the extract from *The Other Side of the Dale* by Gervase Phinn.

What does this extract show about the things the inspector, Gervase Phinn, was looking for when visiting a school?

Give evidence from the text to support your view. *(Higher Tier)*

**4** Look again in The Edexcel Anthology at the extract from *The Other Side of the Dale* by Gervase Phinn.

What impression have you formed of Joseph Barclay from this extract?

You should consider:

❖ his appearance, character and relationships
❖ the language he uses
❖ the knowledge he shows.

Support your answer with examples from the text.

*(Foundation Tier)*

## EXAM TIP

- Identify the key words in the question.
- Spend no more than a few minutes thinking about and planning your answer.
- Begin with an introduction and sum up with a thoughtful conclusion.
- Comment, don't just describe.
- Include relevant examples from the text to support your points.

# C Reading short stories from different cultures and traditions

- There is one question and it will ask you to write about two of the short stories. The question will name either one or both of the stories.
- This question is worth 10% of the overall mark for your GCSE English.
- You must answer the question in 40 minutes.
- Your answer to this question will be assessed against Reading assessment objectives (i) and (v). See page 6.

By the end of this section you will have sharpened four skills that will help you to improve your answer on stories from different cultures and traditions:

1 make the most of your understanding of cultural context

2 comment on characters, don't just describe them

3 focus on the themes and how they connect to character and plot

4 plan to link two stories as the question demands.

You will also explore answers at different grades and assess your skills through writing an answer to a question about short stories from different cultures and traditions, similar to the one you will meet in the exam.

## Stories from different cultures and traditions

The six short stories in the Anthology are rooted in particular cultures or traditions:

- *Country Lovers*, set on a South African farm during the time of Apartheid
- *Veronica*, set in a remote Nigerian village in the mid-20th century
- *The Schoolteacher's Guest*, set in Agua Santa, a remote village in Chile, in the recent past
- *The Gold Cadillac*, set in the USA (Detroit and Mississippi) in 1950
- *A Stench of Kerosene*, set in Northern India in the mid-20th century
- *Vendetta*, set in Corsica and Sardinia in the 1880s.

## What is the examiner looking for?

Below are the characteristics of a good answer and of a weak answer. Find the pairs of comments that match. This activity will focus your attention on the qualities that will gain you marks in this section of the exam. The first pair has been done for you.

| A good answer | A weak answer |
|---|---|
| • writes equally about both stories and links them well | • writes only about one story or offers little on the second story with no attempt to link the two |

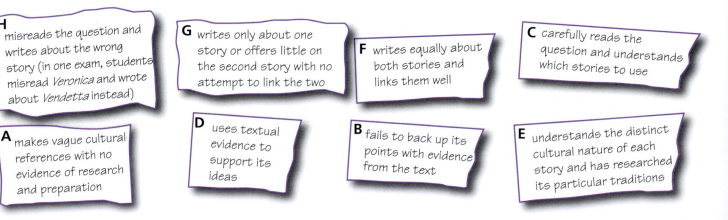

H misreads the question and writes about the wrong story (in one exam, students misread *Veronica* and wrote about *Vendetta* instead)

G writes only about one story or offers little on the second story with no attempt to link the two

F writes equally about both stories and links them well

C carefully reads the question and understands which stories to use

A makes vague cultural references with no evidence of research and preparation

D uses textual evidence to support its ideas

B fails to back up its points with evidence from the text

E understands the distinct cultural nature of each story and has researched its particular traditions

# 1 Make the most of your understanding of cultural context

What does cultural context really mean? Each country referred to in these stories has its own particular culture (or way of life), complete with its own distinctive set of traditions. Some of these countries' cultures have been greatly affected by war and poverty, by strict customs that have existed for thousands of years and by political events. To truly understand these stories, therefore, we need to look at the bigger picture in which they are set. We need to view what is going on within the story in the light of what is going on outside of it. Each story needs to be viewed in its own cultural context.

A good answer shows your understanding of cultural context in relation to what the question is asking, and the importance of cultural context to the story.

Examiners want to see:

- ✓ that you understand how a story's cultural context directly links to the question and that you can use that context to support the points you make
- ✓ more detail about your understanding of cultural context when it is useful to get your point across.

Examiners do not want to see:

- ✗ a few vague references to the culture or traditions of a story that aren't linked to the question
- ✗ long, isolated summaries detailing a particular culture, tradition or cultural point without showing how they support the point being made.

1 Read the exam question below. We are going to focus on the cultural context of just one of the stories it names, *Country Lovers*. Think carefully about the question. What are its key words? What different sorts of 'forces' do you think it is referring to?

---

*Country Lovers* and *Veronica*

Relationships can be destroyed by circumstances and laws. How do the writers show the forces that lead to destruction in the two stories?

In your response you should refer closely to the texts.

---

2 We are going to focus on cultural forces to see the best way of improving your answer. Read the notes below giving some of the background information to this story.

*Country Lovers* is set on a South African farm during apartheid.

In 1948 the National Party began to pass laws to introduce a system of apartheid in South Africa – which essentially meant black and white people were kept totally separate in all areas of life including schooling and marriage.

**Country Lovers – what do you already know about its cultural context?**

The Bantu Education Act (1953) created a school curriculum that gave black people a far more limited education than white people, since it was designed to provide them with the skills to serve their own people in homelands or to work in labouring jobs under the white people.

It was not until 1992 that apartheid was officially abolished.

**3** Read the three extracts from student essays on the cultural context of *Country Lovers*. One is at grade D, one at grade C and one at grade A*.

Match each student's work with the corresponding examiner's comment and decide which answer received which grade.

## Student 1

Paulus and Thebedi's relationship is destroyed by their cultures and traditions. Black and white people were not allowed to mix together outside of work or go out together. Because Paulus and Thebedi have played together since they were children, they see nothing wrong in going out together and even give each other presents. But they swap the presents in secret.

The education for the black and white people was very different. So that meant that Paulus would be better educated than Thebedi and because he gets sent away to school, he is living a very different life from her and knows more things than she does. That's another reason connected to culture that their relationship wouldn't work.

## Student 2

Because the blacks and the whites were not meant to be together there was lynching which happened all the time and this was where the Ku Klux Klan went round killing black people by hanging them from trees and doing other horrible things to murder them and some black people hadn't even done nothing, but often it was said they had gone out with a white person. The gang always wore white pointy hats and face masks and white costumes so that no one would know who they were.

When Paulus finds out the baby looks white not black he changes towards the black girl as he's not nice to her anymore like when he visits her hut he doesn't really talk to her when he is the father after all and it's not fair on the black girl that their different customs means he kills her baby.

## Student 3

Another strong pressure that clearly leads to destruction in 'Country Lovers' is the cultural force which conspires against the couple from the moment their relationship takes shape. Whilst both Paulus and Thebedi are victims of their own culture's traditions and beliefs, Thebedi is clearly the most powerless of these two characters. The 1953 Bantu Education Act effectively suppressed black children and this is highlighted in the way Thebedi is given just enough education so that she can function in village society and the kraal, in direct contrast to Paulus' boarding school education.

Within this cultural context of segregation, their relationship was fated from the beginning. This is also shown by the way the writer presents their changing relationship as the story develops and by the fact this 'short' story actually takes place over a number of years which is unusual for this genre. As young children they play together 'side by side', oblivious to the racial intolerance that exists in their society. As soon as Paulus begins to mature, however, he assumes the role of her master ('He told her...when they would meet again') and later of course takes charge of the crisis surrounding the baby's colouring ('I'll see what I will do').

## Examiner's comment a)

A confident response that shows a good understanding of the characteristics expected in a short story. The student demonstrates a strong awareness of language and effectively links analysis of language with the cultural analysis.

The student interprets Thebedi's character in the light of the cultural backdrop to this story, by focusing on the contrasting educational paths that the main characters follow.

## Examiner's comment b)

This response starts well as the first paragraph opens by immediately focusing on the question. However, it is too vague at times and needs to elaborate on some points. More should be made of its cultural references, for example, why 'black and white people were not allowed to mix together outside of work'.

Paragraph two also opens on a promising note, but again lacks explanation. It attempts to describe 'how' the writer shows the cultural force but needs to explain its points much more fully.

## Examiner's comment c)

Unfortunately this student confuses South Africa with another culture entirely and so wastes valuable time.

The student shows understanding of the way the relationship changes between Paulus and Thebedi, but textual references are lacking. Personal opinion is expressed effectively.

**4** Here is a longer paragraph from a grade A answer, continuing on the same topic. Read it through several times before answering the boxed questions, which will help you understand how an answer like this can be achieved.

| | |
|---|---|
| 1 | Set against the harsh background of apartheid laws, Paulus and Thebedi's |
| 2 | relationship never stood a chance. However, they are both fully aware of the |
| 3 | impact of the apartheid system on their daily lives, that is, whites are seen as |
| 4 | superior to blacks and any relationship between blacks and whites should be |
| 5 | purely professional with no intimacy. Even before their physical relationship |
| 6 | begins, the pair exchange presents without other people knowing: 'he had to |
| 7 | give it to her secretly' and 'She told her father the missus had given these to |
| 8 | her'. Although they try to ignore the cultural pressure '– they squatted side |
| 9 | by side on the earth bank' and subconsciously act as though it does not exist, |
| 10 | as suggested by their symbolic positioning by the river, it is far too powerful |
| 11 | a force to harness. Paulus' sudden arrival at the kraal after the baby is born |
| 12 | and his fierce, mostly monosyllabic questioning and comments that follow 'You |
| 13 | haven't been near the house with it?...Don't take it out. Stay inside' suggest he |
| 14 | has much more to lose than Thebedi. It seems evident that 'word' has got round |
| 15 | of the baby's light colouring and 'fine floss' hair and in this cultural setting, the |
| 16 | shame is too much to bear for him and his family, leading to the suggestion |
| 17 | that he murdered the baby. |

How do lines 1–2 maintain a grasp on the question's key words?

How do lines 2–5 effectively blend cultural knowledge with character analysis?

In what ways are lines 8–11 a good example of using interpretative skills?

Lines 11–14 make a language point about Paulus' words. What point does it make and what does this really show about Paulus?

So how does this answer achieve its high grade? This response:

❖ is insightful and assured – the student has confidently selected the cultural references and uses them for maximum effect

❖ confidently links its understanding of the cultural issues with the couple's fated relationship and perceptively analyses 'how' those forces lead to its destruction

❖ presents a real depth of cultural understanding and uses that knowledge to underline the writer's methods in presenting a relationship that is destroyed

❖ shows perceptive language awareness and links well with the cultural analysis.

Let us focus now on the short story *Veronica*.

**5** Read the spider diagram on the cultural context of *Veronica* and, on the next page, the short extract from a D grade essay focusing on this topic.

Setting: African village (probably Nigeria since the writer has set many of his stories in his native land where he was born in 1953)

**Veronica – what do you already know about its cultural context?**

Time: during mid twentieth century

Cultural backdrop: Nigerian politics were renowned for their extortion and power struggles following the country's independence from Great Britain in 1960. A sharp contrast existed between the few in power who enjoyed wealth and luxury and the majority of its inhabitants who lived in poverty. Regional hostilities continued after independence, and conflict between different groups battling for power led to civil war breaking out in 1967.

> *Veronica doesn't go to the city like Okeke because of her traditions which means she has to stay at home all the time. She's not a man like Okeke so she can't go where she wants because she has to live by the rules that are made up for all women because otherwise her dad will beat her up again.*

To push this answer to a C grade standard, this student needs to:

☑ specify what 'her traditions' are and discuss the impact of these within the story, e.g. Veronica's traditions keep her a prisoner in her own village as she must stay home to cook, clean and look after all the members of her family

☑ discuss the village customs knowledgeably and examine the distinction between male and female roles and futures

☑ support points with textual references.

---

**6** Rewrite the extract to improve its grade. Use the checklist above.

---

**7** Now focus on the short story *A Stench of Kerosene*.

**(a)** Jot down ideas on this story's cultures and traditions in note or diagram form.

**(b)** Then write two paragraphs detailing how its writer shows the cultural pressure that leads to destruction in this story.

**(c)** Swap your work with a partner and use the checklist below to see how they have done. Tick each box that applies as you work through your partner's answer.

**(d)** When your 'marked' answer is returned, make use of your partner's constructive criticisms and this checklist to improve your answer in the areas where it may need strengthening.

---

☑ Has your partner made points about the cultural pressure in the story?

☑ How many times has the question been referred to when making new points?

☑ How many times has textual evidence been used to support points?

☑ Has the use of cultural knowledge been selective and relevant to the question?

# 2 Comment on characters, don't just describe them

When a writer portrays a character in a story, it is usually done in a number of ways so that gradually we are able to build up a bigger picture of that character.

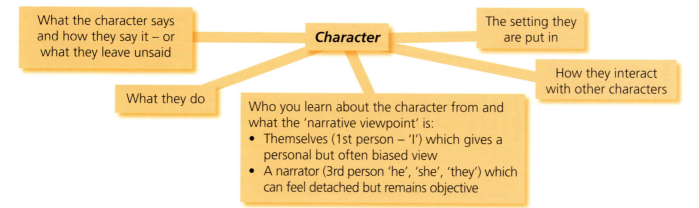

What the character says and how they say it – or what they leave unsaid

**Character**

The setting they are put in

What they do

How they interact with other characters

Who you learn about the character from and what the 'narrative viewpoint' is:
- Themselves (1st person – 'I') which gives a personal but often biased view
- A narrator (3rd person 'he', 'she', 'they') which can feel detached but remains objective

Examiners want to see:

✓ An **objective** evaluation of a character, e.g.
*Veronica, as a woman, is imprisoned by thousands of years of strict customs, which bind her to the village and lead her to accept her fate.*
not a **subjective** opinion, e.g.
*Veronica had the chance to leave her village but stupidly chose not to take it. She could have easily escaped her abusive father.*
By all means give a personal view, but characters are not always straightforward so think about them from more than one angle.

✓ Your understanding of their motives – what makes a character tick, e.g.
*Veronica knows her place is with her family and it is her sense of loyalty and duty which keeps her rooted in the village and drives her daily actions in caring for them.*

✓ Good use of textual evidence to back up your points – refer to the part in the text that made you think your point about the character, e.g.
*Veronica says 'I leave that to others, my own place is here'.*

Examiners do not want to see:

✗ Long descriptions of what a character looks like – physical appearance is usually less important than what the story says about a character's mental, emotional and spiritual characteristics.

✗ Long descriptions of what a character does in the story – the examiner knows that already. Instead use your time wisely to examine why or how a character acts as he/she does.

✗ Points made without being supported by quotations.

*Remember* to make a point about the character or writer's craft if you mention physical appearance, e.g. 'we do not expect such violent emotions and actions from a 'wrinkled' old woman'. This means you are commenting rather than simply describing.

*Remember* not to become blinded by your own personal view of a character.

Look carefully at how it is possible to interpret the writer's words. Do not take them at face value, but dig deeper and think about what else they could really mean. See how small details can be full of meaning, as in Ines 'not even lowering her voice'.

**8** You are going to comment on the character of Ines from *The Schoolteacher's Guest*.

**(a)** Use the character spidergram on page 67 to get you thinking about Ines' character.

**(b)** Read the table below and see how the information in columns 1 and 2 is analysed in the final column.

**(c)** Write your own comments for the two empty comment boxes as well as the whole of the final row with your own point concerning Ines' character.

**Character's Name:** Ines      **Story:** *The Schoolteacher's Guest*

| Description of character | Textual evidence | Comment on character |
|---|---|---|
| She goes into Riad's shop and gives him some unusual news. | 'walked to the counter…announced to him that she had just cut off the head of a guest in her boarding house' | Her behaviour suggests a calm, detached and matter-of-fact manner that is shockingly out of proportion with the act of violence itself. Her coolness is chilling: it is as if she has just announced some trivial, everyday detail. |
| Ines holds a high position in society and people take notice of her. | 'Her authority, in fact, was mightier than that of the priest, the doctor, or the police' | Ines is a very powerful woman and acts as the town's matriarch (female ruler). Her power is far reaching and even surpasses spiritual, medical and criminal authorities. Her word is final on all matters – she is held in high respect by others. |
| Ines does not whisper when telling Riad where the corpse is when a guest is present in the room. | "In one of the back rooms…' not even lowering her voice' | She appears to be neither ashamed of the dreadful act of murder she has committed nor afraid of getting caught or others knowing. She has evidently waited for this moment of revenge ever since her beloved son was killed. |
| She works out how long it will take to clear up the room after the murder. | 'calculating that it would take her two days to wash out the stains and at least two more to rid the room of its odour of faeces and fear' | |
| Ines gives her reason for beheading the man. | 'I had to do it. It was fate.' | |
| | | |

**9** Repeat Activity 8 with three more characters of your choice from the stories in the Anthology. Include at least one main character that you are not so familiar with, as this will help you deal with whatever story (or stories) may be named in the exam.

**10** Look again at *Veronica*. Reread the conversation between Veronica and Okeke on the second half of page 72 in the Anthology, just before Okeke leaves for university. We learn a great deal about Veronica's character during this dialogue. Look now at the examples of student responses to this part of the story below and read the examiner comments.

## Grade A response

Okeke's first question to Veronica 'What about you?' prompts a genuinely shocked response 'Me!' She is so used to putting others first that she cannot possibly imagine leading a life solely for herself. Veronica is a product of her own culture, one where women are subservient to men and exist to serve them and look after their family members, 'I can't just leave my family.' Her sense of duty to her family is extremely strong. Many centuries of tradition have moulded her into this submissive existence and she becomes defensive when her position is challenged by Okeke. Veronica's view of life is fatalistic and Okeke's character is used here to further contrast the difference between their futures, since he feels both 'appalled and frightened' by her acceptance of her own fate and complete lack of desire to change it. Using Okeke to provide the narrative point of view clearly affects how we view Veronica and their relationship, as outside of their conversations we lack her real thoughts and feelings. So certain is she of her own future, however, she actually mocks Okeke's attempts to change her fate 'Don't talk foolishness'. The expectations of those around her hold her firmly in place.

> This answer begins by commenting on character immediately, with an excellent point on what Veronica's language says about her character

> This is a good evaluation of the impact of tradition on the character

> Here the student shows awareness of the limitations of using 1st person narrative to portray Veronica fully

> The student demonstrates a good understanding of Veronica's fatalistic attitude to life

## Grade D response

When Okeke and Veronica talk to each other before he leaves for university, she tells him that she will not leave her family 'I can't just leave my family.' No matter what he says or does she does not change her mind. I think that in her society, family means everything and women were not supposed to go off and get an education or leave their village or do anything like that. I do not think her dad would let her anyway, as we know he abuses her, by hitting her. It's annoying that Okeke will not take no for an answer, typical man, as she says time and time again no to him but he just will not listen. So she ends up laughing at him, probably hoping that if she takes the mickey out of him he will leave her alone.

> Avoid repetition when quoting like this

> This is a good point – but what does it suggest about her character? This part of the answer is too vague and lacks depth of response

> Avoid slang in your essay and use formal language instead, e.g. 'makes fun of', not 'takes the mickey'

**11 (a)** Now write your own response to this conversation, focusing on commenting on Okeke. Use the examiner comments above to help you.

**(b)** Swap your finished answer with a partner and:
- underline parts where there are comments on Okeke's character
- circle parts where Okeke's character has just been described.

If you have any descriptions, look at how you can turn them into comments.

## 3 Focus on the themes and how they connect to character and plot

To answer a question on themes well, you need to be familiar with the different themes that present themselves in the six short stories and think about different ways of comparing them.

> **12** For each story in the Anthology, write a list of relevant themes from the spider diagram below. (Remember, some themes will be used more than once and each story will have several themes.)

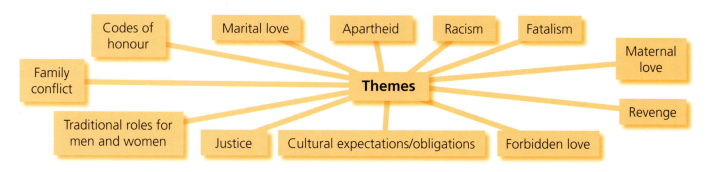

In the same way that it is important to comment on and not just describe characters, you need to comment on and not just describe themes.

> **13** Read the following question which focuses on themes, and then read what the examiner expects in your answer.

> Both *Vendetta* and *The Schoolteacher's Guest* deal with ideas of justice and revenge.
>
> How do you think the writers show the personal and cultural forces that lead to characters taking their revenge? Refer closely to the texts.

**Examiners want to see:**

☑ An essay that focuses on the key words. What are the key words in the question above?

☑ Comments on the techniques the writers use to present the personal and cultural forces that lead to revenge. For example, in *Vendetta* the writer shows the old woman's grief through the use of alliteration in 'silently shedding great tears'. The mother's grief is an example of a personal force.

☑ A balanced answer – in the case of the question above, this means giving equal weight not only to both stories, but also both sets of personal forces and cultural forces.

☑ Your personal opinion – do not be afraid to give this.

☑ A link between the two stories at some stage.

☑ Points being backed up by references to the text.

**Examiners do not want to see:**

☒ A simple, descriptive summary of the personal and cultural forces that leads the characters to take their revenge.

☒ An imbalanced answer or focusing on only one part of the question or just one story.

☒ No effort to link the two stories.

☒ Points being made with no textual back up.

**14** Read the following three short paragraphs discussing the mother's love and grief in *Vendetta*.

  **(a)** Put these paragraphs in grade order, giving reasons for your choice.

  **(b)** Now match the student responses to the examiners' comments.

### Student 1

The widow is really sad about the death of her son and it seems she loved him a lot as she calls him 'my little son' but at first she finds it hard to cry, which is usual I think when someone close to you dies. She just stands looking at him for a long time, until she cannot take it any more and bursts out crying. I think it is this sadness that makes her want to kill the man that did this and this is why she tells him not to worry and that she will get the man that killed him.

### Student 2

In 'Vendetta', a strong personal force that drives the widow into action is that of maternal love, which the writer portrays as unconditional and absolute. 'Gazing' at the corpse, the widow is presented in an extremely sympathetic light, even though we realise this persistent gazing also serves as a potent reminder of his violent death and will spur her on to carry out the (probably equally violent) vendetta. Despite this, we still begin to pity her for her loss and the obvious suffering it has caused her, suggested by her 'silently shedding great tears'. The image of her final goodbye kiss 'pressed her cold lips to the dead lips of her son' is indeed chilling and reflects utter devotion. Furthermore, her dead son is portrayed as a small boy once again, and ironically as a child to be protected forever by its mother 'my son, my little son, my poor child'. By using a pattern of three to repeat the possessive pronoun 'my', we are reminded of that maternal bond and deep-rooted grief which has resulted from his untimely death.

### Student 3

One personal force that leads the widow into taking her revenge is the depth of the love she feels for her son as his mother, which the writer shows in different ways. One way is by repeating the word 'gazing', as she keeps looking at his dead body covered in blood. The memory of his blood-stained body will always remind her to carry out the vendetta as she will never be able to forget this awful sight. The way in which she talks to his dead body is also very sad and makes us feel sympathetic towards her, 'You have your mother's word and you know she never breaks it.'

### Examiner's comment a)

This response definitely grasps the point of the question but falls into the trap of mostly just describing the 'personal forces' but failing to expand upon its points. Textual evidence is minimal but there is an attempt at interpretation in the final line.

### Examiner's comment b)

This response has moved towards comment. The key words of the question are repeated, which link the answer directly to the question and give it a confident direction. Language evaluation is present, such as the reason for the repetition of gazing, but there was scope for more, which would have added insight to this response. Personal opinion here is well presented.

### Examiner's comment c)

This is the most perceptive of the three paragraphs. It provides a confident analysis, with a mature focus on the writer's use of language. Quotes are used purposefully and points are made in a precise manner.

## Cultural forces

The examiner wants to know *why* revenge is so important to the widow and what methods the writer uses to present it.

**15** Write one paragraph on the cultural forces that lead the widow in *Vendetta* to taking her revenge. Make sure you think about the distinct culture and family traditions of Corsica and Sardinia at that time, which lead the old woman into issuing her vendetta, and how they are presented in the story, for example, the way language is used to convey these ideas.

When you have written your paragraph, swap with a partner and use the examiner comments above to check how well you have discussed the cultural forces. Is there anything that can be improved?

**16** Now apply what you have learned about commenting on themes to *The Schoolteacher's Guest*. Write a paragraph on the personal forces that lead Ines to take her revenge and a further paragraph on the cultural forces that lead her to do so. Use the examiner comments above to check how well you have analysed the forces. Is there anything that can be improved?

# 4 Plan to link two stories as the question demands

A good answer will show that you have structured your essay to ensure you link the stories.

Two main methods are usually used to link the two stories.

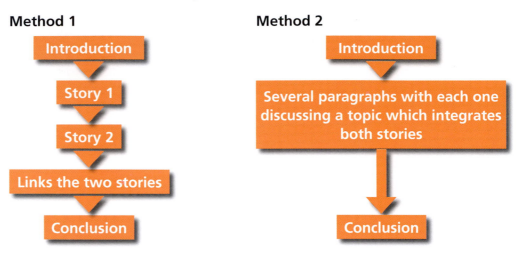

**Method 1**

Introduction → Story 1 → Story 2 → Links the two stories → Conclusion

**Method 2**

Introduction → Several paragraphs with each one discussing a topic which integrates both stories → Conclusion

**EXAM TIP**

It is your choice which method you use. The examiner will value both methods equally.

The main difference is that Method 1 is structured in a more straightforward way as each story is initially discussed separately before being linked (in terms of similarities or differences) in the conclusion. Method 2 'juggles' both stories throughout the answer and consistently refers to both.

**18** Using the ideas from Activities 15 and 16, you are now going to use the format of Method 1 to write two short paragraphs on one cultural point from *Vendetta* and *The Schoolteacher's Guest*, followed by one linking paragraph. Before you start, read the examples which follow from a Grade D answer, a Grade C answer and a Grade A* answer.

## Grade D

'Vendetta' talks about revenge a lot because the widow's son has been killed for no reason so she wants to get her own back on those that did it. She hasn't got a husband any more or any more sons so she's got to do it on her own but she doesn't do it on her own because she gets the dog to do it in the end.

Ines in the other story gets revenge because her son is killed for no real reason so she waits and waits until one day the murderer comes back into town so she hacks him to death.

Both these women are mothers and both lose their sons and so both kill the men that killed their sons.

## Grade C

In Italy when someone was killed it meant their honour was not respected, so that is why the old woman in Vendetta wants to kill her son's killer. This is a tradition which had been going on for years so she is just following the customs and says 'You shall be avenged'.

In the other story Ines wants revenge and so waits for the right moment to kill her son's killer as she says 'I had to do it'. It's more the villagers who want revenge when it happens though because they go mad when they hear what's happened to her son, so the cultural force comes from them really.

The two mothers more or less do the same thing for the same reasons, but in 'Vendetta' the old woman seems to plan it a lot more and seems to want it to happen much more because of her culture.

**Grade A\***

*The cultural force which leads the old woman to take revenge in 'Vendetta' is shown very clearly. Corsica and Sardinia were famous for their blood-feuds at that time. The widow's son's honour has been hugely disrespected and her quest to restore it surpasses any law in her eyes since she effectively takes the law into her own hands. This is shown quite clearly by the repetition of the widow's words to her dead son's corpse 'Never fear, never fear, you shall be avenged...You shall be avenged'.*

*In 'The Schoolteacher's Guest', the focus of the honour which has been disrespected is not so much concerning the dead boy or Ines, but the villagers, who feel openly outraged by the murder. This story clearly focuses on a group effort. This is portrayed by their frenzied, ritual-like attack on the murderer's house with fruit 'spent the day hauling mangoes' and is further heightened by the respect with which Ines is held in the town and by the fact the murderer is 'an outsider'.*

*Codes of honour, therefore, in 'Vendetta' and 'The Schoolteacher's Guest' are extremely important to both the female main characters and add great momentum to their quests for revenge.*

Although each of these responses achieves a different grade, they have all used Method 1 to structure their work, which makes their points easy to follow.

**19** Look again at the exam question below (you partly worked on this in Activity 2, page 63). Using what you have learnt, complete the activities below.

    **(a)** Plan your answer focusing especially on how these two stories can be best linked for maximum marks. Use Method 1 (discussing each story separately and then linking them) or Method 2 (integrating the stories as you discuss each point).

    **(b)** Using your plan, write a full response to the question. You have 40 minutes.

    **(c)** When you are finished, use the checklist below to see how well you have done and to make any improvements necessary.

---

*Country Lovers* and *Veronica*

Relationships can be destroyed by circumstances and laws. How do the writers show the forces that lead to destruction in the two stories?

In your response you should refer closely to the texts.

---

☑ Clear initial focus on the direction your paragraph is going to take.

☑ Enough cultural context included to support your point.

☑ Both stories discussed at equal length concerning your point.

☑ Both stories linked at some point during your essay (Method 1) or during your paragraphs (Method 2).

☑ Textual evidence used to support your ideas.

## D TO C

Notice how the grade C answer on page 72 uses textual evidence to support its points. Quotations must be used to back up your ideas.

- The C grade gives more detail that the D grade and attempts to explain its points more fully.

- The D grade shows a basic understanding of what the question is asking. The C grade goes one step further showing more awareness of the key words in the question and attempting to refer to them during the answer.

- The C grade doesn't just say 'the two stories are the same' but points to differences between the two, as well as similarities.

## B TO A

- Analytical and interpretative skills are required at this level, as well as the ability to appreciate and evaluate alternative interpretations of the short stories.

- Cultural understanding is perceptively expressed and firmly linked to the key words of the question.

- New points are developed in detail.

- Textual evidence usually consists of brief quotations which are skilfully worked into the point being supported.

You are now going to pull together all the learning from this section by attempting a complete essay answer to a question on *The Gold Cadillac* and *A Stench of Kerosene*. You will then study two other students' answers for comparison.

**20 (a)** First answer the question below. You have 40 minutes.
**(b)** Then read the student answers and examiner comments below. Complete the activities in the boxes.

Look again at *The Gold Cadillac* (Anthology pages 79–85) and *A Stench of Kerosene* (Anthology pages 86–88).

To what extent do you think that Wilbert and Manak are responsible for the difficulties or tragedies that occur in the two stories?

Refer closely to the texts in your answer.

### Student 1

> This is a confident opening, showing the examiner the essay's direction.

1 I think that Wilbert is totally responsible for the difficulties that occur in 'The Gold Cadillac' and that Manak is half responsible for the tragedy that occurs in 'A Stench of Kerosene'. Both Wilbert and Manak know that there will be trouble because of their actions, but only Wilbert is man enough to do anything about it.

5 I think that in 'The Gold Cadillac' Wilbert is totally responsible for the danger he puts his family in. The first reason I think that is because he gets far too carried away about how lovely the new car is so this makes him forget the trouble he could get into if he drives it south. He couldn't resist buying it 'I just couldn't resist it!' and he says this to one of the men who lives near him. And he also likes it

> Do not directly repeat your quotations like this.

10 because all the other men and women around who see it seem a little jealous of him as they wish they could have one too as the story tells us they all admire the Cadillac.

> This paragraph lacks textual evidence. Which quotations would you choose to improve it?

The second reason I think that Wilbert is mostly responsible for the danger he puts his family in is because he feels lots of pride that he can own it, even though he's not

> This essay has a repetitive structure, clearly indicating that new points are being offered in each paragraph.

15 a white man. One of his aunts tells him not to worry his wife doesn't want to ride in it straight away because soon she will feel proud of riding in it and Wilbert agrees with her so that he hopes his wife will soon change her mind and then she will not be angry with him anymore.

My third reason why I believe Wilbert is responsible is because he must have

> This 'third reason' is also lacking in textual reference. Which relevant quotation could be included here?

20 known what would happen if he drove that fancy car down south to the area where there was lots of prejudice. In those days the whites thought they were better than the blacks and treated the blacks like slaves, so if he drives it down south and is caught by a white man, that white man will think he has stolen it and he will be in loads of trouble. He should have known better really, especially as he is a dad and

25 a husband and has got two kids and a wife to look after.

> This is a well-argued point.

My fourth reason why I believe Wilbert is responsible is because he should have acted like a man and stood up to his wife and told her no, she could not go down south with him. He was probably secretly pleased that she finally wanted to ride in it I think. He did actually tell her 'No!' but he should have said it more and put a

30 stop to her idea.

In the end, Wilbert realised he did something wrong and this is why he changed the cars in the story and carried on his journey but in an older, dirtier car. This proves he is responsible I think and at last he owned up to his mistake as he says to his wife 'it's just not worth the risk'. I think he means the risk of his family getting picked up again by the police and being treated horribly for doing nothing. It wasn't fair the way he got treated because he wasn't hurting anybody, just driving in his new car.

I am now going to talk about the next story that I have studied. In 'A Stench of Kerosene' Manak is half responsible for what happened to Guleri but I think his mother in law and the traditions they have to live by are also to blame.

My reason for saying this is because he doesn't want to talk to her about the fair she is going to with her friends. I think the real reason for this is because he knows he won't be going to visit her at the fair as the second wife is coming, and he knows that when she does return she'll be really mad and really upset that he's got a second wife because they are supposed to be in love. This quote shows that they love each other 'they had bartered their hearts to each other'.

Manak's mum I think is also partly to blame for the tragedy because she is horrible to him as she has a go at him the minute he gets back indoors and is rude to him as she says 'Why do you croak like an old woman?' There's a really important quote which blames the mum 'Obedient to his mother and to custom, Manak's body responded to the new woman but his heart was dead within him.' It's the mum who thinks their family custom is so important and so it's her that brings the new woman in. Basically, their tradition says that a married woman must give her husband babies and because Guleri hasn't had a baby in seven years, this has vexed his mum. She probably worries that all the people in the village are talking. But we know Manak doesn't want to be with the new wife because he feels dead inside – he's missing his real wife. It's easy for people to say he should have stood up to his mum, but that's not always easy and they don't know the ins and outs of it. Some mums are so wearing the trousers in a family their sons don't stand a chance.

I know Manak or his mum or the culture didn't kill Guleri themselves by pouring the kerosene on her, but it was because of all of them together that she killed herself really. Wilbert and Manak are quite similar in the stories because both of them lead their loved ones into trouble, but I think Wilbert did this more deliberately than Manak, especially since he was warned by those people around him what could happen but he was stubborn and went ahead and did it anyway. Manak just had to do what he was told and had no choice in the matter. He was a mummy's boy I think.

This paragraph forms an effective signal that the student is changing story, with a hint of the direction the answer will take. Overall, how effectively have the stories been linked, in your opinion?

This section is mostly descriptive. How could you develop the points being made about who is responsible and why?

Good recognition of significant textual reference

Although there are some valid points, the language is very colloquial. How would you rewrite these points in a more formal style?

A thoughtful conclusion

## The examiner's view

This essay shows a sound understanding of each character's responsibilities and offers a range of relevant points, distinguishing between difficulty and tragedy. The comments on the main characters and the extent of their responsibilities are interesting and well-made but there are also examples where opportunities for further exploration are not taken. The essay is clearly structured, although repetitive in its layout. The student does not give many textual references, however, and at times the language used to express ideas is too colloquial.

**A good grade C answer**

21  Assess your own answer against this C grade answer. Look at the 'Steps to success in reading' on page 7 to check how well you are meeting the assessment objectives. What do you need to work on to improve your grade?

**Student 2**

An immediately firm grasp of both stories indicates to the examiner where this essay is heading.

This essay uses Method 1, i.e. it deals with one story at a time.

The student mentions the cultural context and then explains how it is relevant to the point being explored about the text. Find another place in this essay where the student has made good use of cultural context before examining an idea.

This use of rhetorical questions here and below to present important points on the family's safety is effective.

The student gets side-tracked a bit here and spends too much time discussing the daughter when making this valid point. Rewrite this paragraph editing the parts that you feel may be irrelevant to the question.

This balanced paragraph shows that the student is aware of more than one way of interpreting the story before giving a personal opinion.

This is a perceptive comment on character. Find another example of such a comment in this essay.

Signals that the next story is now being discussed.

1 'The Gold Cadillac' is set in the 1950s when there was a great deal of racial discrimination. Wilbert did know of these problems but he drove the Cadillac anyway. In 'A Stench of Kerosene' Manak knew what would happen but he enabled her to leave anyway. He did not know that she would die, however.

5 In 'The Gold Cadillac' I think he is partly to blame for the difficulties that occur. When he brings the car home there is excitement within the whole community. If he has worked hard and can afford a car then he should be able to have it and drive it freely. The mother's reaction however stands apart from the rest. 'You didn't buy this car, did you, Wilbert?' She realises the implications of having this
10 car within their community. In the 1950s the black community were seen to be inferior to the white Americans. Therefore they were often seen as not only poor but also untrustworthy. Wilbert is obviously aware of the black/white divide and he did already know the risks when he purchased the car.

The narrator, who is the daughter of Wilbert, is very excited by the car; this
15 shows her childish pride and materialism: 'driving up to the church in that gold Cadillac and having everybody see.'

Wilbert obviously is very proud of the car and likes the effect it creates. I feel that he could have been responsible for the events if there had not been so much prejudice at that time. However, he was fully aware of the extent of this
20 prejudice, and when he drove south he knew the implications. Despite this, he put his family under danger. His materialism got the better of him, which is a failing on his part. Is the safety of his family not more important to him?

Although the narrator loses innocence within the story, I think it is good that she learns how the real world is. This experience was necessary for her education,
25 since you never really understand and appreciate something unless you experience it yourself. She now understands how corrupt people are, but finds this a frightening discovery. 'There was a long, sharp knife in the picnic basket and I took hold of it.' This shows that he has directly put his family in danger and scared his daughter. She is petrified of what might happen. As a father it
30 was irresponsible of him to put her under this pressure; she is frightened to sleep, even. Surely her safety is more important than a car?

Wilbert undoubtedly showed a kind of bravery in not conforming to the community in which he lived. However, the fact that he put his family's safety in danger is ultimately more important. At the end he realises that material
35 possessions are indeed less important than his family and sells the car. This highlights how he has grown as a person from the experience as he now realises his own responsibility: 'We all rode in it together, and we were a family again'.

In 'A Stench of Kerosene' Guleri is desperate to go home for her annual visit, as she is isolated from her friends and family. She does not, however, realise what
40 will happen when she does go home this harvest-time. Manak is aware of what will happen and tries to convince her to stay, but she does not want to.

'Blew a strange anguished wail.' I think this highlights the extent to which he wants to stop her going, since his soul seems to be crying out to her to stay. Guleri however is excited to go home as she has been at the mercy of Manak's mother and wants to see her family. Because of the cultures and traditions in the community, Manak just let the following events happen. He does not fight for Guleri to stay; instead he lets her go, out of respect for his mother.

I think the responsibility for the events is not entirely down to Manak, because of the culture and traditions of the society he lived in at the time when the story was set. The importance of having children was such that love was far less highly regarded in a marriage. 'I am not his wife...I am just someone he happened to marry.' This is what the new wife says about her relationship with Manak. She is aware that he does not love her, but within their community that is acceptable.

Manak and Guleri fell in love and were able to marry. The irony is that he wanted to give her a family of their own but was unable to do so. In the end his family betrayed Guleri and she killed herself because she could not face the disgrace and the fact that he had taken a new wife into the family. Manak was trapped within the expectations of his society; there was little he could do. He was 'obedient to his mother and to custom'. He could have gone after her or insisted on being with her, but he still obeyed his mother. 'Manak's body responded to the new woman but his heart was dead within.' He has no deep feelings towards the woman; it is a mechanical relationship.

The remorse he feels at the end of the story, I think, shows his love for Guleri. However, to have stayed with her would have gone against his own society and his mother: they would have had to disown themselves from the culture and move somewhere else. This would have been quite unacceptable to his mother. She just tells him to 'be a man' and accept his responsibility to provide an heir. Love was less important than tradition and duty. It was these traditions that led to the tragedies in the story. However, Bhavani, Manak's friend, makes him feel 'uneasy'. Manak feels the 'other man's rebuke' and so the reader has to see that there is some feeling of guilt in Manak.

Both stories show the powerful effect of traditions, and how individuals cannot simply do what they like because of what other people think. But the men have to own up to their own responsibility and Wilbert definitely does this more than Manak.

Line numbers: 45, 50, 55, 60, 65, 70, 75

*Margin notes:*

There is some excellent language analysis here.

The student's character analysis is backed up by knowledge of cultural context.

The student shows a full awareness of both sides of the central issue.

Notice that this paragraph contains constant references to the key words of the question with brief and apt quotations.

The conclusion pulls together the main points of the essay well, but is weak in linking the two stories together. Rewrite it to link the two stories together more effectively.

## The examiner's view

The response is very full and detailed. It examines both men in their social and cultural context, and there is a very good attempt to evaluate the extent of their personal responsibility for how things turn out. In the writing about *A Stench of Kerosene*, well-argued points are made about the weight of tradition bearing down on Manak. The structure of the essay, however, meant that the candidate made very few links between the two stories. Perhaps the student panicked at the end as time was running out.

**A grade A answer**

> 22 Assess your own answer against this A grade answer. Look at the 'Steps to success in reading' on page 7 to check how well you are meeting the assessment objectives. What do you need to work on to improve your grade?

## 6 Exam question practice

Now is the time to put everything in this unit into practice for yourself.

*Remember* that
you cannot practise too
much. Areas such as
making the most of your
understanding of the
cultural context, analysing
characters rather than just
describing them, focusing
on the meaning of the
different themes and
using planning to link the
two stories will improve
very quickly.

### EXAM TIP

- Spend no more than a
  few minutes thinking
  about and planning
  your answer.
- Begin with an
  introduction and sum
  up with a thoughtful
  conclusion.
- Comment, don't just
  describe.
- Include relevant
  examples from the text
  to support your points.

**23** Allow 40 minutes, and choose from the questions below.

When you have finished, assess yourself against your answer to the
question in Activity 20, or swap your work with your partner and assess
each other's. Look back at the 'Steps to success in reading' on page 7 to
identify exactly where you are doing well and where you need to improve.
Note down three areas in which you would like to improve, and practise
those skills.

**1** In The Edexcel Anthology look again at *The Schoolteacher's Guest*
and *Vendetta*, both of which deal with revenge.

What do you find interesting about the part played by the mother
in each story?

You should consider:

- ❖ the events which lead the mothers to take revenge
- ❖ the methods of revenge which they use
- ❖ their backgrounds
- ❖ their ideas of what is right.

Support your answer with examples from the text.

*(Foundation Tier)*

**2** Some of the stories look at relationships between men and
women. How are the women presented in these stories? In your
answer refer to *Veronica* and ONE other story from The Edexcel
Anthology. You should consider:

- ❖ the women's backgrounds and education
- ❖ their relationships with men
- ❖ their relationships with children
- ❖ words and phrases used to describe the women and their lives.

Support your answer with examples from the text.

*(Foundation Tier)*

**3** Some of the characters in these stories take the law into their own
hands. Do they deserve respect or condemnation for their actions?
In your answer, refer to *The Schoolteacher's Guest* and ONE other
story from The Edexcel Anthology.

Give evidence from the texts to support your views.   *(Higher Tier)*

**4** Look again in The Edexcel Anthology at *Veronica* and *Country Lovers*.

Relationships can be destroyed by circumstances and laws. How do
the writers show the forces that lead to destruction in the two stories?

Give evidence from the texts to support your views.   *(Higher Tier)*

# D Writing to inform, explain, describe

This section will help you to improve your answer to this writing question. You will sharpen three skills that examiners say are important for good grades:

1 identify the purpose of your writing – to inform, explain or describe

2 organise and present your answer effectively

3 use language to communicate clearly and in detail.

You will then explore the qualities of answers at different grades and assess your skills through writing an answer to a question that is similar to the one you will meet in the exam.

## Writing to inform, explain and describe

When you write to inform, explain and describe:

◆ you are focusing on giving information to the reader

◆ sometimes you give very factual information; sometimes you give detailed explanations

◆ common forms of writing are letters, leaflets, media scripts (e.g. radio), autobiographical writing and newspaper articles.

## What is the examiner looking for?

Below are the characteristics of a good answer and of a weak answer. Find the pairs of comments that match. This activity will focus your attention on the qualities that will gain you marks in this section of the exam. The first one has been done for you.

### IN THE EXAM
### SPECIFICATIONS A and B

■ There is one writing task. You can choose from two questions.

■ The writing task will test your skills in writing to inform, explain and describe.

■ This question is worth 10% of your total mark for GCSE English.

■ You must answer the question in 40 minutes.

■ A third of the marks for this question are awarded for using a range of sentence structures effectively, and for accuracy of punctuation and spelling.

■ Your answers to this task will be assessed against Writing assessment objectives (i), (ii) and (iii). See page 8.

| A good answer | A weak answer |
|---|---|
| • uses paragraphs to present the information in a clear way | • includes lots of information in no particular order |

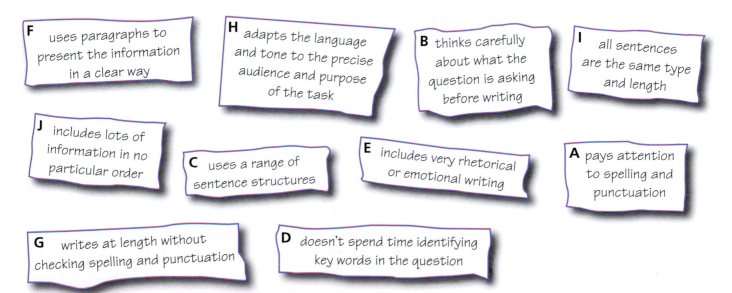

F uses paragraphs to present the information in a clear way

H adapts the language and tone to the precise audience and purpose of the task

B thinks carefully about what the question is asking before writing

I all sentences are the same type and length

J includes lots of information in no particular order

C uses a range of sentence structures

E includes very rhetorical or emotional writing

A pays attention to spelling and punctuation

G writes at length without checking spelling and punctuation

D doesn't spend time identifying key words in the question

When you write to inform, explain or describe you are giving information to the reader.

❖ Writing to **inform** is very factual.
❖ Writing to **explain** goes into more detail about how you do something or why something is the case.
❖ Writing to **describe** often involves giving an account of a place, person or event.

## Writing to inform

When you write to inform:

☑ avoid waffle – your response should be factual and relevant
☑ use clear and direct language
☑ structure your response carefully to guide the reader through the information.

> **1** Some students have been given the task of informing each other about the route they take to school. Read the two responses below, and imagine that you are the examiner. Write a comment on each of the features in the checklist above, explaining why the grade indicated has been awarded.
>
> You may like to begin like this:
> *Student 1 has included some facts, such as ... but they are not always relevant, for example ... The language is ...*

*Remember* to think carefully about the precise purpose of the task. You must adapt your language and tone to that purpose. Emotional writing, for example, is usually not suited to a task that asks you to inform, explain or describe.

### Student 1 (Grade D)

*I come out of my front door I say goodbye to my mum then I turn left down springfield road and I often meet my friends who live along that way so we walk together and chat. We talk about what we did the night before and things like that and what we are going to do at the weekend when there is no school. I cross the road and carry on until I see the fish and chip shop then I know I'm nearly there. We get fish and chips from there every Friday they do the best fishcakes in the area and my dad can eat five in one sitting. I think they are closing down soon as they have lots of competition in that road from others and you can see our school from there.*

### Student 2 (Grade C)

*My house is on Brompton Road so when I leave it I turn right for about half a minute, then I cross over Laxton Way using the zebra crossing at the bottom and carry on to the bottom of Brompton Road for another minute before turning left into Riverfield Drive. There is a big park on your left of this road and several houses on your right. Then I walk forward for about another minute down this road and then I come to the school's entrance, which has a big blue sign saying 'Rowena High School'.*

*Remember,* sometimes you will be asked to give information in a more lively way. For example, you could be writing a brochure giving information about local attractions to tourists. This kind of writing should include more descriptive language.

**2 Either**

Rewrite Student 1's response to push it up to grade C. To achieve this you would need to:
■ remove the irrelevant information
■ correct sentence structure (some sentences are very long) and punctuation.
**Or**
Rewrite Student 2's response to push it up to grade B. To achieve this you would need to:
■ improve the choice of words (two uses of 'big', for example)
■ vary sentence types (three uses of 'then' – how could that be avoided?).

Make sure you pay attention to the comments you wrote as an examiner in Activity 1.

# Writing to explain

When you write to explain, you are giving a clear and detailed account of a situation. You are explaining why or how something is done, or how someone does something. Some important features of writing to explain are:

- ☑ It takes a logical and step-by-step approach.
- ☑ The language is clear, but also lively and interesting.
- ☑ Examples and detail are given to fill out the explanation.
- ☑ The structure is clear, and 'signposting' words are used to guide the reader.
- ☑ Technical terms can be used, but some must be explained.

**EXAM TIP**

Don't rely too heavily on factual detail at the expense of interesting and lively writing. A technical, long-winded explanation of how email works (for example) is not required for the exam question on this page.

**3** The exam question below focuses on writing to explain. Read the extracts from the beginning of a student's answer. Then answer the examiner's questions in the boxes.

> The producer of a radio programme for retired people is trying to bridge the generation gap by inviting teenagers to talk about an aspect of their lives that older people may find difficult to understand.
>
> Write the script for a short talk that you might give, explaining the importance in your life of ONE of the following: email and texting; music; fashion; or a topic of your own choice.

**Grade A answer**

*From an early age, I have lived in different countries and moved around different schools, due to my father's job. The saddest part of this constant upheaval has been losing contact with all the good friends I made. Of course, I always intended to make the effort to write to them, but somehow I never got round to it. Nothing substitutes for the daily banter, laughs and jokes we used to share. Nothing that is, until email came along ...*

The plan for this essay began like this:
*Life before email: little communication with friends*
*Life after email:*
Complete this plan to show how it gave the essay a clear and logical approach.

*Almost overnight those friendships began to flourish and grow. The snippets of gossip, the everyday adventures and the trials and tribulations of teen life that I used to share with my friends are now all just a mouse click away. No longer do I have to sit waiting for the postman to bring me my next instalment of life in my former neighbourhood. No longer do I have to ransack my dad's bureau, hunting for an airmail envelope or aerogram. No longer do I have to join the back of the long Post Office queue for overseas stamps behind the scores of pensioners who got their act together that morning and got there first!*

Lots of 'signpost' words and phrases have been used to guide the reader e.g. 'From an early age', 'Of course', 'Almost overnight'. Find two others and comment on how they help the reader.

This writing is lively and interesting. How does the student use repetition effectively?

The student includes several examples to give more detail to the explanation. Find three of these examples.

*With one click, we can not only keep each other up to date with our lives, but also send photos and even audio visual snippets. Unfortunately, however, I have discovered the hard way that email attachments (pictures or documents you can literally attach to an email) are not the preserve of the young: my mum delights in sending my friends embarrassing video clips and photos of me!*

The student has explained the technical term 'attachments' here, because the audience may not know it.

**4** Now it's your turn to try writing to explain. Write two paragraphs in response to the exam question above. Use the checklist of features above to guide your writing.

# Writing to describe

Here are some of the features and techniques of descriptive writing.

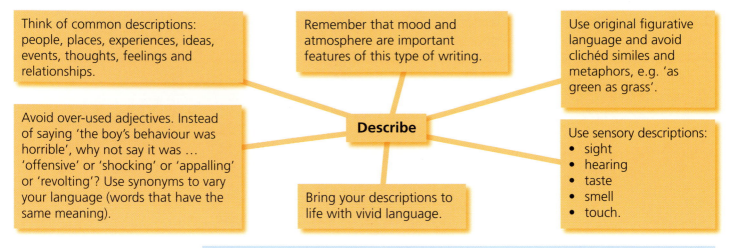

Think of common descriptions: people, places, experiences, ideas, events, thoughts, feelings and relationships.

Avoid over-used adjectives. Instead of saying 'the boy's behaviour was horrible', why not say it was … 'offensive' or 'shocking' or 'appalling' or 'revolting'? Use synonyms to vary your language (words that have the same meaning).

Remember that mood and atmosphere are important features of this type of writing.

**Describe**

Bring your descriptions to life with vivid language.

Use original figurative language and avoid clichéd similes and metaphors, e.g. 'as green as grass'.

Use sensory descriptions:
- sight
- hearing
- taste
- smell
- touch.

**5** Look at the exam question below, then read the three extracts from students' responses and the examiner comments.

**(a)** Match each comment to the correct student extract.

**(b)** Then give each student extract a grade: one is A, one C and one D.

(Hint: refer back to the spider diagram above and think about which extracts have made good use of the descriptive techniques described there.)

> You are a refugee living in a strange and new country. Write a letter to relatives or friends back home, describing to them what your new life is like and what challenges you face.

**Student 1**

> I feel alone though: the people here seem so materialistic and concerned about conforming to the normal. There are unwritten social rules about what to wear, who to be friends with, how to talk. Despite my longing to stay in this country, I do not fit in. It is hard, I'm not seen as the 'perfect image' of what a woman here should look like. They have long groomed hair; mine is a matted mess. They have well-nurtured bodies; mine is scrawny and weak. They have manicured nails, mine are stubs at the end of my fingers, showing the world my untold history.

**Student 2**

> Oh Kumar I feel really lost without you because people don't understand my accent and because I look so different from everyone else I need you here to translate for me like you did when we watched those english tv programmes together. My day is really hard I have to get up really early and I'm treated like a dog and the sewing machines are really noisy and I can barely hear myself think as they make a loud noise all day long from the moment I arrive to the time I go home so please come and get me because I really don't think I can go on like this.

**Student 3**

> Rana, everytime I close my eyes before I go to sleep I imagine that I'm back with you and the rest of the family in the warmth of our hut and that we are all gathered around the fire. I can't stand the chilling cold days and the dark depressing nights as my life is so very hard here and I really do feel like a fish out of water. I don't speak the language properly and so don't have any friends. My room is as small as a matchbox and smells like a mouldy sag aloo!

**a)** At times, it is difficult to follow the meaning because of the lack of punctuation. More full stops and commas are needed.

**b)** The reference to ethnic food, with its original simile, is a good attempt to make the letter more authentic.

**c)** This extract insightfully portrays life in a foreign country as a refugee and tries hard to engage some of the five senses, e.g. sense of touch and sense of smell.

**d)** Alliteration is used twice in one sentence to good effect. Two other similes, unfortunately, are commonly heard ones and so do not add to the originality of this piece.

**e)** The language used is rather simple and straightforward – there are several places where a detailed description could have improved this piece.

**f)** This candidate successfully bases the description in her paragraph on various oppositions. The visual contrast she describes is both striking and powerful, with the added use of a triple alliteration to emphasise the extent of the difference.

**g)** An original metaphor in the final line is very effective and compels us to read on to find out more. A truly engaging description.

**h)** This candidate's descriptions need to be more original and lively. Her words feel tired and repetitive.

**6** Read the following extract from a teen penpal website. Stefanie is trying to describe her interests and personality. However, the writing is very factual and dry, and there is not enough detail. We do not get a sense of who she really is.

**(a)** Stefanie would get a D for her description. Look at 'Craft your answer' in the margin. Where does Stefanie fall short in achieving grade C?

**(b)** Rewrite her description to boost her grade.

---

**E-Pals Cont@ct**

I'm a college student, studying a 2 year course in A Level Travel and Tourism. I enjoy reading, going to the cinema, watching DVDs or listening to music. I'm also interested in animal welfare and would love to contact like-minded people.

Stefanie, 17, London (*stefinlondon@hotmail.com*)

---

## D TO C

To move from a D grade to a C you need to:

- **Craft your answer.** Don't just write the first thing that comes into your head. Write down your thoughts and order them so that they have the most effective impact possible on their reader.

- **Control your sentences and paragraphs.** Don't forget the basic rules: every sentence begins with a capital letter and ends with a full stop, question mark or exclamation mark. Begin a new paragraph when you move on to a new point.

- **Be brave with your language.** Try out a new simile or metaphor, for example, instead of resorting to tired old images or clichés.

- **Bring your writing to life.** Think about how you can appeal to the senses in your descriptions.

- **Improve your spelling.** Now is the time to list those words you usually spell wrong and learn them properly.

## Why form and structure are important

When you are presenting information, you need to think carefully about the form and structure of your writing. In particular:

✓ Are you taking the correct form of the writing into account? If you are writing a letter or newspaper article, for example, this needs to be clear in the structure and language.

✓ Can you start with a good introduction? This could be a clear statement of the issue, or a lively opening that grabs the reader's interest.

✓ Can you organise your points in a logical order? You should give a separate paragraph to each one.

✓ Can you show the reader where your writing is going? This means using 'signposting' words and phrases.

✓ Can you round the writing off well at the end? A good ending shows that you have thought about the overall structure and effect of your writing.

**EXAM TIP**

In the exam you should remember to use greetings and sign-offs that are formal (Dear Sir ... yours faithfully; Dear John ... yours sincerely) or informal, as appropriate, but you need not normally include your address or the date at the top of the letter. The examiner is interested in whether you can write in appropriate tone and style, rather than in the details of setting the letter out.

**7** Read the exam question below, and the beginning of two student responses. Answer the questions in the boxes.

A local newspaper has invited readers to write in with ideas on how to improve facilities in the community for young people. Describe your plans in a letter to the newspaper, and explain how these would meet the needs of young people.

### Student 1

Correct form (polite letter) used. How would this student end the writing?

'However' is a good signpost word showing that a contrast is about to be made. What purpose does the signpost 'It is for these reasons' indicate in the next sentence?

How does the final sentence show the reader (and examiner) what the rest of the letter will consist of?

> Dear Sirs,
>
> Having lived in the same community my whole life, I have grown up around the same people and have used the facilities that are already on offer in this region. However, as you grow older your needs change, and although when you are at nursery school a set of swings and a roundabout will just about satisfy your social needs, the case is different when you develop into a young person. It is for these reasons that I have proposed plans to develop facilities for young people in this village and the surrounding areas.

What makes this opening paragraph a clear and effective introduction to the letter?

**Student 2**

How does this heading show that the student hasn't thought about the form of the writing?

The response launches straight into an attack on the council. Does this make a good introduction? Give your reasons.

*My ideas for facilities*

*There is nowhere to go nowadays so it's not our fault if we end up in trouble. The council should provide us with things to do or somewhere to hang out, or it's obvious we're gonna get bored. My cousin Jimmy got picked up by the police last week for breaking a car window, now if he had a ==youth club== or somewhere to go that wouldn't have happened would it? A ==youth bar== selling soft drinks would be good ==as well==. I'd go there and I know me mates would.*

Two good ideas for facilities are put forward here. Could they be placed more effectively somewhere else in the letter? Give details/reasons.

This is a good signposting phrase, showing another example. Add a signpost to the sentence beginning 'My cousin Jimmy'.

This paragraph begins with a general point, then gives an example. This is a good way of giving your points structure. Rewrite the last two sentences as a new paragraph that follows the same pattern: general point + detail/example.

## Planning

If Student 2 above had drawn up a simple plan, it would have helped a great deal in boosting the grade of the answer. Many of the faults highlighted above are the result of not having a plan.

The simplest kind of plan has only three basic steps.

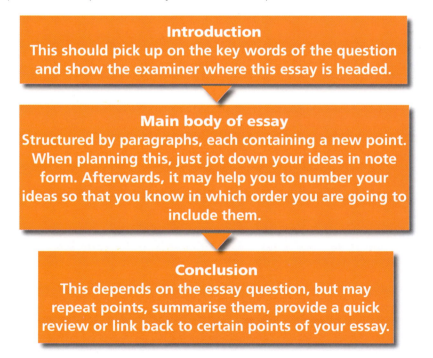

> **Introduction**
> This should pick up on the key words of the question and show the examiner where this essay is headed.

> **Main body of essay**
> Structured by paragraphs, each containing a new point. When planning this, just jot down your ideas in note form. Afterwards, it may help you to number your ideas so that you know in which order you are going to include them.

> **Conclusion**
> This depends on the essay question, but may repeat points, summarise them, provide a quick review or link back to certain points of your essay.

**8** Write a plan for Student 2's essay, using the basic approach outlined in the chart above.

# 3 Use language to communicate clearly and in detail

When you write your answer, you need to think carefully about the tone you are using, and how you can make your language interesting.

## Getting the right tone

Tone refers to the mood or atmosphere of your writing. The tone you use for your answer will depend upon the audience, form and purpose of the task set.

Common tones you might adopt include the following:

light-hearted     angry     descriptive     warm

emotional     informal     serious     detached

**9** How many more tones can you think of to add to the above list?

**10** Look back at Activity 3 (page 81).

The student has used a warm, friendly and at times humorous tone. Find examples of this. How does this tone match the purpose and audience of the task?

**11** Look at the four exam questions at the end of this section (page 91). For each one, make brief notes on the tone that you would adopt in your response.

**12** Look back at the exam question in Activity 7 (page 84).

**(a)** Which of the following tones could you use in your answer? (There may be several.)

*humorous, respectful, serious, emotive, highly personal, objective, balanced, sarcastic, formal*

The tone of Student 2's response on page 85 was not appropriate. It was too aggressive (e.g. the accusations in the sentences at the start) and informal (e.g. the slang).

**(b)** Write your own answer to the question in the appropriate tone, using the plan you wrote for Activity 8.

## Making your language interesting

Interesting writing:

- ✓ makes use of different types and lengths of sentence
- ✓ uses powerful words and imagery (especially in writing to describe).

---

### Remember

**Imagery** refers to the writer's use of an image or picture to describe something. Common forms of imagery are:

- similes, where something is compared directly with something else, e.g. 'He stood as solid as a mountain'
- metaphors, where terms used to describe one thing are used to describe another, e.g. 'He wasn't so much a mountain – he was a volcano which occasionally erupted'.

### EXAM TIP

The examiner will be looking for a range of different kinds of sentence in your writing. So vary the lengths of your sentences, and include questions and commands or exclamations among the statements. Using punctuation effectively can help you write longer and more varied sentences.

**13** Reread the exam question below (seen before in Activity 5). Here are three further extracts from student responses. Which ones have made the most effective use of language techniques and different types of sentence?

**(a)** Read the examiner's comments and match them to the correct extract.

**(b)** Grade the extracts C, D or A.

> You are a refugee living in a strange and new country. Write a letter to relatives or friends back home, describing to them what your new life is like and what challenges you face.

## Student 1

*Don't leave me here Sunil! I will never get used to the strange customs in this foreign land as every night I sit in my room, tears rolling down my cheeks, rocking back and forth on my bed wishing myself back to my old life. P l e a s e. Help me.*

## Student 2

*Monday 18th April*

*The traditions here are really strange because at a time they call easter which someone told me was about being a christian person they give each other*
- *chocolate eggs*
- *furry rabbits*
- *the children wear special hats at school with eggs and baby chicks on them*

*and even funnier the children go hunting for them as they hide them. It's got something to do with a rabbit but that doesn't make sense.*

## Student 3

*I try to make friends and I do have a few, but most turn their noses up at socialising with me. Why wouldn't they? I do not conform. I refuse to. Never. You know my strong nature! Yet I cannot get myself heard. I'm that unnoticed whisper from the back of the crowd. The pathetic one who's been shipped over here, invading their homes. I always thought that my personality would get me far in life, but here it seems that the exterior is more important. Such shallow souls.*

## Examiner's comment a)

Whilst this candidate's vocabulary is rather limited, there are some positive features. The use of a diary format works well, as we imagine other 'good' or 'bad' days to come, but the lack of punctuation makes it difficult to read.

## Examiner's comment b)

This begins well with an emotive plea and makes good use of an imperative to reflect the level of distress involved. The image of the writer sitting in a room is a strong one and begins to work on our sympathies at such a plight, but more powerful language could have been used here to describe the desperate feelings. The spacing of 'please' along with the two short sentences at the end add variety to the sentence structures.

## Examiner's comment c)

Clearly an accomplished and polished piece. The rhetorical device and pattern of three short or one word sentences add great impact at the start. A powerful metaphor in the middle commands the reader's attention and lifts the writing. The alliterative ending adds a moral viewpoint that we could easily identify with.

**14 Either**

Rewrite the D grade extract to make it a C grade.

**Or**

Rewrite the C grade extract to improve the grade further. Focus on the sentence structure and language features.

## 4 Work with student answers

You are now going to pull together all the learning you have done in this section by attempting a complete essay answer. You will then study two other students' answers for comparison.

**15 (a)** First answer the question below. You have 40 minutes.

**(b)** Then read the student answers and examiner comments below. Complete the activities in the boxes.

> Describe a person who has impressed you or been a strong influence in your life, bringing out the key characteristics that make him or her special for you.
>
> You may choose someone you know personally, or someone you have heard or read about.

### Student 1

> Does this make a good introduction? Give your reasons.

1 Nanny Olive died just over a month ago now. She was 91. No one in my life has ever been a big influence over me like that and I don't think anyone ever will as she was the life and soul of every party and her bright eyes and big smile I'll sadly miss.

> This student tries to use some interesting words, e.g. 'scoff', but some of the phrases are not original, e.g. 'out of the blue', 'fit as a fiddle'. Rewrite this paragraph avoiding clichés and focusing on making the language more powerful.

5 It came out of the blue really as she'd only just been to my birthday party the month before fit as a fiddle trying to beat us in the sack races. I'd better explain about them that's my mum's fault as she still insists we have our little sports day, my brother and me and our friends after we've scoffed all that birthday food! Anyway there was Nan as usual trying to 10 knock my friends over with her walking stick but pretending she was talking to Auntie Jean.

> This student knows how to use paragraphs to organise the ideas. What is the topic of each paragraph?

It was two weeks later we'd heard she'd had a fall at home. In hospital they did tests and soon realised it was cancer and it didn't take long to spread from her body to her brain but anyway I won't dwell on that bit. I've got 15 heaps of happy memories to remember her from.

> This student has some good ideas, but the punctuation and control of sentences let them down. Rewrite this paragraph to boost the answer's grade.

She knows I'm not that keen on school but she always encouraged me to do my best in my exams and to do my homework Sometimes she would even do it for me as I'll never forget the time my maths teacher asked me about my method of long division as teachers changed their methods after the 20 second world war.

She lost granddad really early on, from that same rotten disease. And she never complained about being lonely, she taught me about how important it is to have your family around you and if you've got your family around you then you've always got someone to talk to.

25 I wouldn't call her a skinflint but another thing she taught me was about being careful with money I guess because she's had to survive all those years on a pension. I don't have much anyway but what I do have I've learnt now to put by for a rainy day nan used to say.

> We scattered her ashes outside the bingo. Mum made me do it (she gave
> me what she called danger money) and I had to pretend I'd dropped my
> 30 school bag so I could get enough time to get the lid off the coffee jar we'd
> put them in. Those urn things they give you are really big. Nan would have
> liked that as she called it her second home. She was always looking on the
> bright side as she was always saying one day she'd win the big money on
> 35 the live link up. She never did of course.
>
> I'll never forget my Nan. She was always there when I had a fight with mum
> or dad and when a teacher had had a go at me that day for being late
> (she was still working on my punctuality). If I turn out with just a few of her
> many qualities, I won't have done too bad in life.

This student has thought carefully about the tone of the writing. It is both humorous and sad in places – identify one example of each.

## The examiner's view

The content of this essay is very readable but it isn't always presented in the best possible way. It is lively and quite humorous in places, and we get a real sense of the loss felt, but the candidate would make a greater impact by incorporating some more linguistic or structural features. Too many slang words are used, as well as clichéd phrases such as the simile 'fit as a fiddle'. Although we get a good sense of Nanny Olive, the descriptions themselves could have been much tighter and more detailed. The sentences lack punctuation in a number of places which results in ideas running into each other, making it difficult to follow in places.

**A good grade C**

> **16** Assess your own answer against this C grade answer. Look at the 'Steps to success in reading' on page 9 to check how well you are meeting the assessment objectives. What do you need to work on to improve your grade?

### Student 2

> 1 One of the people who has had a huge influence on my life is someone who I
> have never met and never will. He was my Great Uncle, and he died in 1944.
>
> I don't know Joseph, and my grandfather rarely speaks of him. But a
> collection of letters, kept in my family for over sixty years, have allowed me
> 5 to build up a sense of his character, and a great admiration for him.
>
> Joseph died fighting in World War II, like so many other young men. He
> was nineteen when he died, only a few years older than me. Yet while my
> problems revolve largely around not having enough money to buy the
> clothes I want and dealing with school work, he spent many of his teen
> 10 years just trying to survive.
>
> Reading his letters, the thing that I am most struck by is his amazing
> bravery. He faced fear that I cannot comprehend, and ran headfirst into
> situations more dangerous and terrifying than I will ever have to face. And
> yet he never complained, never wanting to let on to my great grandmother
> 15 that he was afraid. His hope, courage and even sense of humour in the face
> of such awful circumstances astounds me, and makes me realise just how
> much I, and indeed, my generation, take for granted.

This is a very simple introduction – can you explain why it works so well?

'The thing that I am most struck by' is a good signposting of what this paragraph is going to be about. What signposting does the student use in the next paragraph to guide the reader?

What is the topic of each paragraph? The first sentence usually tells you.

**20** Apart from his bravery, it was Joseph's consideration for others that really amazed me. In a war situation, surely our instinct for self-preservation should take over. But not in Joseph's case. His letters were full of concern for others – his comrades, his family back home. 'I'm doing this for you', was the closing sentence of one of his letters. It was said with no trace of bitterness, not even a real sense of pride. He was just reminding his family, as I'm sure he often had to remind himself, why he was there, and what he **25** was fighting for.

The writer has a thoughtful tone throughout, relating personal values here to those of the great uncle. Where else does the student do this in the essay?

What Joseph went through, and his attitude towards it, has changed the way I think about my own life. It has made me feel stronger, and more able to achieve my goals – looking at what he went through, I feel it's my duty to enjoy the life and opportunities that I have been given.

**30** I believe that we learn greatly by studying the actions of others, and understanding Joseph's actions, and the choices that he had to make, has changed the way I think. I strive to be more like him and do what is right without hesitation.

If Joseph could rise above such horrific situations, I know that I can rise **35** above whatever problems I may face. To the rest of the world he is just one in thousands, another anonymous soldier who gave his life for us. But to me, he is a model of what we should all try to be.

What makes this a good conclusion?

Throughout my life, I will hold on to Joseph's memory, the memory of a man I never knew. And I shall treasure the gift that he has given me **40** without even knowing it – he has helped to make me a better person.

## The examiner's view

The candidate has created great interest in the character of the unknown relative, who was not known personally to the writer because he died fighting in World War II. The writing is very sensitive in the portrait it presents, and the language used is fully appropriate to the topic. This is a well-expressed response, relating the writer's personal values to those of the uncle. It is also well constructed and signposted for the reader, showing careful planning. To gain a grade A*, the candidate would need to give the opening more of an impact, show a richer vocabulary and use more varied sentence structures.

**A grade A answer**

> **17** Assess your own answer against this A grade answer. Look at the 'Steps to success in writing' on page 9 to check how well you are meeting the assessment objectives. What do you need to work on to improve your grade?

# 5 Exam question practice

Now is the time to put everything in this section into practice for yourself.

**18** Allow 40 minutes, and choose one of the questions below.

When you have finished, assess yourself against your answer to the question in Activity 15, or swap your work with your partner and assess each other's. Look back at the 'Steps to success in writing' on page 9 to identify exactly where you are doing well and where you need to improve. Note down three areas in which you would like to improve, and practise those skills.

**1** 'My room.'

Write a letter to a friend who has never visited you, giving information about the room you spend most time in.

You should:

❖ describe what this room is like
❖ explain what you think of it
❖ say how you would like to improve it.

*(Foundation Tier)*

**2** 'Hopes and dreams.'

Write a letter to a friend, setting out your hopes and dreams for yourself and the future.

*(Higher Tier)*

**3** For a teenage magazine, write an article with the title: 'How I would like to be treated'.

You should write about:

❖ the feelings you have about this topic
❖ why you feel the way you do
❖ what you would like to do to improve how you are treated.

*(Foundation Tier)*

**4** 'Entertaining relatives: heaven or hell?'

Write a magazine article, drawing on your own, or your friends', experiences, explaining how to make things go as well as possible and pointing out what should be avoided.

*(Higher Tier)*

## EXAM TIP

■ Spend no more than a few minutes thinking about and planning your answer. Are you writing to inform, explain or describe?

■ Use paragraphs and signposting to guide the reader.

■ Vary your sentence structure and punctuation, and check your spelling.

# E  Reading media texts

## IN THE EXAM
### SPECIFICATION A

- There is one question, based on one or more texts.
- You may have to compare texts.
- The first time you see the text(s) will be in the exam.
- This question is worth 10% of your total mark for GCSE English.
- You must answer the question in 40 minutes.
- Your answer to this question will be assessed against Reading assessment objectives (i), (ii), (iii), (iv) and (v). See page 6.

By the end of this section you will have sharpened three skills that will help you to improve your answer to the media question:

1 understand the key features of media texts

2 comment on how media texts use language and layout

3 make clear and relevant comparisons between media texts.

You will also assess your skills through answering questions about media texts that are similar to the ones you will meet in the exam. You will then explore the qualities of answers at different grades.

## Reading media texts

'Media' is the word to describe sources which give us news, information, entertainment, advice and so on. It can be in many forms, including newspapers, magazines, television programmes and websites. The exam question will present you with a printed media text. This might be an advertisement, feature article, brochure, leaflet or mailshot.

## What is the examiner looking for?

The question on media in the exam will:

❖ usually be introduced by the word 'How' or the phrase 'In what ways'. This is to help you focus on analysing the way the text is written and presented

❖ ask you to write about how the purpose of the text is achieved through the use of language and visual presentation

❖ give you a number of bullet points, which will list aspects of the text you need to think about in your answer.

Below are the characteristics of a good answer and of a weak answer. Find the pairs of comments that match. This activity will focus your attention on the qualities that will gain you marks in this section of the exam. The first one has been done for you.

| A good answer | A weak answer |
| --- | --- |
| • focuses on the key words of the question | • summarises/describes the passage |

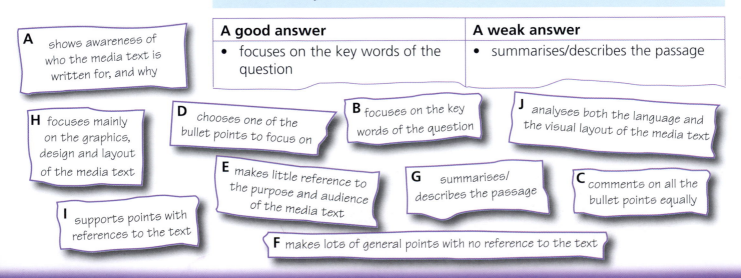

A  shows awareness of who the media text is written for, and why

H  focuses mainly on the graphics, design and layout of the media text

D  chooses one of the bullet points to focus on

B  focuses on the key words of the question

J  analyses both the language and the visual layout of the media text

E  makes little reference to the purpose and audience of the media text

G  summarises/describes the passage

C  comments on all the bullet points equally

I  supports points with references to the text

F  makes lots of general points with no reference to the text

It is important to focus on three key aspects when responding to a media text:

1  **purpose** and **audience** – remember that these are different for each text

2  the ways in which **language** is used

3  **layout** and **design** – in other words, what the text looks like.

## Audience and purpose

1  Read the four media texts on pages 93–95. Think about why they were written (their purpose) and who they were written for (their audience).

Choose the most appropriate audience and purpose in each case from the lists on the right. (Note: each text may have more than one purpose).

## Keep warm, keep moving

Moving around generates extra body heat, so any kind of activity will help to keep you warm.

Don't stay sitting still for long periods.

Spread chores out through the day so you can alternate between rest and activity.

Moderate exercise, such as walking, has real health benefits if you do it regularly all year round.

Try to keep your exercise up in winter, without taking risks in wet or icy weather

### keep moving

9

**FREEPHONE 0800 085 7000**
TEXTPHONE 0800 085 7857

*Remember* that you could be given any kind of media text in the exam. To answer well, it is important to recognise the kind of media text you have been given and comment on it with understanding. Examiners will expect you to know the key features and the correct terms to describe them.

**Purposes**

describe

persuade

advise

inform

analyse

review

entertain

argue

recount/narrate

**Audiences**

adults

elderly people

parents

young people

women

politicians

# FirstNews *Headlines*

## BOMBS HURT KIDS

Children in Lebanon are being hurt by cluster bombs, even though the fighting stopped weeks ago.

Cluster bombs release lots of smaller bombs when they explode. They may not all blow up immediately but land somewhere else unexploded. Children can then pick them up not knowing what they are.

In the last few years many countries and peace groups have demanded cluster bombs be banned. They say they should never be used near homes or schools, or anywhere children could find them.

There are rules that have to be followed when different groups are fighting a war but some people are worried that Israel or Hezbollah broke some of the rules in the recent fighting.

# The useful thing would be teaching them how to read

By **Edward Enfield**

(Father of Harry, who created Kevin the Teenager)

The first time I saw that chap Charles Clark I thought he was crackers. Either I was right or he is like Estelle Morris – the job of Secretary of State for Education is too much for him and he has flipped.

Either way I have rarely seen a bigger load of demented rubbish than he has just issued to the world at large.

He is concerned, it seems, that there are teenagers who cannot boil an egg, change a light bulb or clean a bathroom. There are 15 other things he has been worrying about, such as whether teenagers can put up curtains or mow lawns. Why on earth, I wonder, is the man in charge of education preoccupied with such trivia?

To establish my own credentials, I wish to say that I have experienced the teenage years five times in total; once on my own account and then as the father of four children – one of whom, Harry, was the creator of Kevin the Teenager himself.

For years I used to return from a hard day at the office to find the peace of our home shattered by the noise of filthy pop music. The grunts, the sighs, the sulks – how they all come back to me!

As any parent – or indeed any TV viewer familiar with my son's comic creation – can testify, teenagers are proud to be 'Kevins'.

The Clarke list of 18 basic activities that youngsters should master by the time they turn 16 has, as far as I can see, all the ingredients for the terrible rave-up they would almost certainly arrange if you went away for the weekend.

I imagine it would be interpreted as follows:

'Changing a light bulb or fuse' – installing strobe lights in your living room and fixing up kit to thump out throbbing music and keep the neighbours awake.

'Cooking a simple meal' – feeding the punk horde invading your house.

'Administering first aid' – to those who have passed out by the end of the party.

'Using a washing machine' – to try to get the mess off the chair covers.

'Working the central heating system' – to try to dry the covers over the radiators.

'Decorating a room' – in the hope of covering up the mess on the walls.

'Putting up curtains' – after they have been pulled down.

'Putting up a shelf' – after it has been pulled down.

'Cleaning a bathroom' – don't even think about the state of the bathroom.

'Mowing the lawn' – in the hope that you will be pleased and not notice the mess in the house.

Mr Clarke's list also includes 'making a journey with two modes of transport'. As far as I can see, teenagers are much too good at that already.

I see them all the time with their feet on the seats of trains or sprawled on the seats of buses.

Of course it may be that the teenagers of today are particularly stupid, but I think they are only stupid at intelligent things, like reading books.

The useful thing would be to teach them to read, to write grammatically, to speak articulately and to do not-too-difficult sums in imperial and metric units.

If they could do all that, employers throughout the nation would be overjoyed and the economy would boom as never before.

## Language and layout

When you are analysing media texts, you need to think about the features of language and layout in the charts below. Remember to explain in your answer why a particular technique, word, font has been used. Simply identifying without comment will not achieve a high grade.

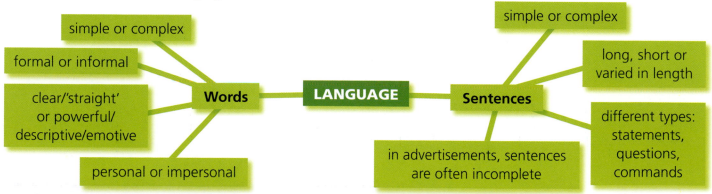

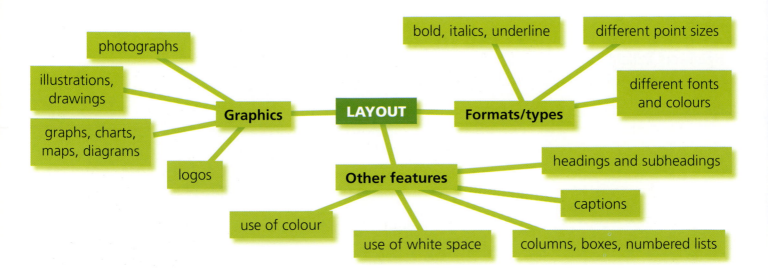

photographs

illustrations, drawings

graphs, charts, maps, diagrams

logos

**Graphics**

**LAYOUT**

bold, italics, underline

different point sizes

different fonts and colours

**Formats/types**

headings and subheadings

captions

**Other features**

use of colour

use of white space

columns, boxes, numbered lists

**Remember** that the media text(s) you are given could be almost any type of writing – advice, argument, news story, analysis, review … You need to know the key language features for each type of writing, so that you can comment sensibly on them.

**2** Choose one of the media texts on pages 93–95 and draw up a list of three language features and three layout features. Give the evidence from the text. Your list may start as shown below.

| Language features | Layout features |
|---|---|
| commands, e.g. 'Keep warm' | Photo of elderly woman |

**3** Compare your list with that of a partner who has chosen a different text. Can you explain any similarities and differences in your lists? Discuss how the features suit the purpose and audience of your text.

When you comment on the language and layout of a media text, you need to keep in mind the purpose and audience of the text.

**4** Read these extracts from two students' answers on the media text 'Bombs Hurt Kids' (page 94). Which one has given more thought to the audience and purpose, so is well on the way to a good grade?

**Student 1**

The language and layout of this news article are very basic. The headline 'Bombs Hurt Kids' doesn't really tell you anything – does it mean they always hurt kids, or they have just hurt some kids? We do not find out until we read the text. The writing is rather dull and factual. It would improve the argument if some more powerful words or rhetorical devices were used.

**Student 2**

The language and layout of this article are carefully considered. The headline is very simple and direct, as the audience (young people) needs to be attracted immediately by its message, and not be put off by any long words. The text is very clear and straightforward. Several aspects of the war are explained, such as cluster bombs, so that the readers are not lost. The emphasis is on getting the information across.

# 2 Comment on how media texts use language and layout

The impact of a printed media text depends on a combination of the **language** used and the **visual features** of design and layout. In this unit you will be looking in more detail at how you comment on these key features.

## Commenting on language

Commenting on language means:

❖ analysing the effect the language has on the reader

❖ referring closely to the text.

> **5** Read the exam question below. Notice how you can identify the **audience** and **purpose** of the text by reading the question carefully.

Read the leaflet 'Riding skills'. How does this leaflet use language to advise young motorcyclists on riding safely?

This shows the purpose of the text.

This shows the audience of the text.

So you need to think about the language features of advice texts. You should also take account of who is reading this advice – young people.

**EXAM TIP**

When you read the exam question, look out for the key words that tell you what the purpose of the media text is, e.g.

*How does the article* <u>present information</u> *about bananas and their benefits?* → an information text

*In what ways does the article* <u>encourage</u> *readers to take a holiday in Spain?* → a persuasion text

---

## Riding skills

To keep out of trouble YOU'VE GOT TO BE GOOD. If you're already good, make yourself better. The best motorcyclists ride defensively so they are less likely to have accidents. We all meet idiots on the road and motorcyclists are vulnerable to their mistakes. Those with good defensive skills ride like they expect to meet one every second. They are in control, so they enjoy more relaxed riding.

Make sure you:

• **Anticipate** the actions of motorists.

• **Are alert and observant.** Important when you are negotiating junctions or roundabouts; and when you need to look out for other vulnerable road users – children, pedestrians, cyclists and horseriders.

• **Ride at a speed that will enable you to slow down** and stop in good time. The unexpected can happen. And ride according to the conditions: slow down if it's wet, foggy or icy.

• **Position yourself in the best place.** Usually the middle of the lane. But take up your road position in good time before turning right or left, showing others what you aim to do.

• **Overtake safely.** Can you see hazards? Is there a bend or a junction? Can you overtake without speeding up or swerving too much?

• **Take a 'lifesaver' glance over your shoulder** before carrying out manoeuvres when you need to know where other drivers are and what they are doing.

• **Are seen.** Dipped headlights, even in good daylight, can help you to be seen.

Sometimes other drivers will wind you up. But if you act aggressively you may have to pay the penalty. Count to 10 and congratulate yourself on your cool-headedness. And however tempted you are, don't race on public roads. Save it for the race track.

If you want to know more, read the Driving Standards Agency publication Motorcycle riding: the essential skills. You can also take advanced training. There are different schemes to suit your needs.

**6** Copy and complete the grid begun below to show how the language features of the text give advice to young motorcyclists. Add your own examples and comment on why the writer has chosen each feature. Then add any other language features you notice, with examples and a comment.

**Remember** when you are commenting on language to:

- focus on the key words of the question
- 'flex your PECs': point – evidence – comment
- think about all aspects of language: words, sentences, paragraphs, tone, style
- always bear in mind the audience and purpose of the media text.

## EXAM TIP

You will always be asked to comment on the language of the media text. But don't forget that you will also be asked to comment on other features as well, such as layout.

| Point about the language feature | Example | Comment – why is this appropriate? |
|---|---|---|
| direct, straightforward words | *To keep out of trouble you've got to be good* | <ul><li>advice needs to be clear and to the point</li><li>using simple words means everyone can understand it</li></ul> |
| use of commands or instructions | *Position yourself in the best place* *Overtake safely* | |
| informal, conversational language | | |
| positive language | | |
| other features | | |

**7** When you have chosen your features, examples and comments, you need to put them together in a good answer. Here are the openings of three students' answers. Match them to the correct examiner's comments. Then list them in order of merit, with the best one first.

1 *This leaflet gives advice clearly. I agree with it.*

2 *This leaflet uses the imperative form of the verb, for instance 'Overtake safely.'*

(a) Good opening sentence which establishes a platform for developing other points. The point about language is made clearly, with appropriate use of technical language and brief, effective quotation.

(b) This just 'feature spots' – it gives an example but no explanation, and provides no link with the question.

(c) This consists of a simple statement and a personal opinion.

3 *The language used by the leaflet is skilfully directed at a largely male and teenage audience. Colloquial words like 'idiot' and phrasing like 'sometimes other drivers will wind you up' suggest a no-nonsense approach that will speak directly to young male readers.*

**8** Now write your own answer to the question 'How does this leaflet use language to advise young motorcyclists on riding safely?'

# Commenting on layout

Commenting on the layout of a media text means:

❖ analysing the graphics and the way the text is presented on the page

❖ referring closely to the text in your answer.

These are similar to the skills that you use when commenting on the language. Again, you should keep the audience and purpose of the text in mind.

**9**   Read this extract from an A grade answer. The student is commenting on the graphics used in the leaflet 'Riding Skills'. Answer the questions in the boxes.

Graphic devices are used to good effect in this leaflet. To begin with, there are several small photos of riders. These are intended to engage the interest of the young people so that they will read the leaflet. They are small because the main purpose of the text is to give detailed advice, but to make up for this, there is a sophisticated background image of a motorcyclist. This is hazy, and may even suggest a crash, so it gives the 'other side' of riding that the leaflet is aiming to avoid.

The colours used in the leaflet are also carefully chosen – mainly blue, with touches of orange. The overall effect is sober, which suits the subject matter, but also attractive. The designer did not want to take too much attention away from the text, being aware that the young male readership is easily diverted!

The student makes it clear what types of graphics are being talked about. A **general statement** about photos comes first, then further **details** are given. Show how this pattern is repeated in the second paragraph.

The student is taking the **audience** of the text into account. Find another example of this.

Note how the student uses the Point – Evidence – Comment approach skilfully. Identify the PEC in the 2nd paragraph.

The student refers to the **purpose** of the leaflet here. Find another example of this.

**10**   Read this D grade answer, which is commenting on the way the text is presented in the same leaflet. Improve its grade by (a) using the techniques you have identified above, (b) thinking about the examiner's comments in the boxes below. The writing is too informal in places.

The writing is mostly in boxes, the boxes are dark green which matches the title, there's one box for each bullet as well which is quite cool, in fact the more you look at it the more boxes you see, eg the boxes round the photos. Also bullet points are used – these are little round dots that start each line. The writing is black except for when its white. Some of it is orange so it stands out. The black stuff is all a bit dull.

The student could improve the answer by giving a **general overview** of the features first.

How could the student **organise** the answer better?

No need to explain what bullet points are! Instead – what is their **purpose** and **effect**?

More **reference to the text** is needed.

All media texts are different, depending on their purpose and audience. Advertisements for the same kind of product will vary: for example, an advertisement for a breakfast cereal aimed at children will be different from one for a breakfast cereal aimed at adults who are concerned about their health. A serious newspaper will present a news item in a different way from a popular newspaper.

In the examination you may have to **compare** media texts. This means you have to:

☑ write about the ways in which the texts are the *same*

☑ bring out the key *differences* between the texts

☑ *explain* and *comment* on these similarities and differences.

> **11** Below are the characteristics of a good comparison answer and a weak comparison answer. Find the pairs of comments that match. The first one has been done for you.

| A good comparison will | A poor comparison will |
|---|---|
| • focus on the question | • say everything there is to say about the media texts |

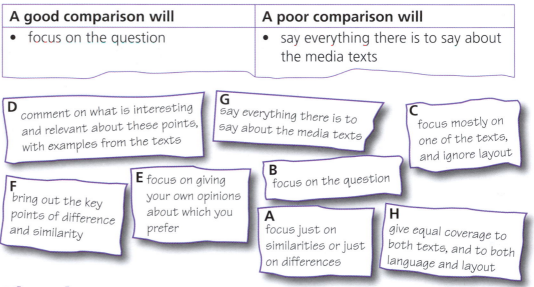

**D** comment on what is interesting and relevant about these points, with examples from the texts

**G** say everything there is to say about the media texts

**C** focus mostly on one of the texts, and ignore layout

**F** bring out the key points of difference and similarity

**E** focus on giving your own opinions about which you prefer

**B** focus on the question

**A** focus just on similarities or just on differences

**H** give equal coverage to both texts, and to both language and layout

## Planning your answer

> **12** Read and study carefully the following exam question and the two newspaper articles about the same hamster on the next two pages.

> Compare the different ways in which the *Sun* and *Guardian* newspaper articles present the story of the hamster's escape to interest and entertain their readers.
>
> In your answer you should consider the following points:
> • content – what each article includes or omits
> • design including graphics
> • use of language
> • tone.

# Pet's terror trip through industrial recycler . . and lives to tell the tail

**2** He passed along a conveyor belt and through a giant shredder, which can tear a cooker or washing machine to pieces in seconds

**3** He rodent then survived a rotating drum and vibrating grids

**4** Astonished staff discovered the hamster in a sorting area and he only had an injured paw

**1** The hamster found its way into a skip of rubbish that arrived at a recycling plant in Flintshire, north Wales

# SHREDDY PLANT ATE MY HAMSTER

**A HAMSTER** got carted off in a rubbish skip to a recycling plant — and survived being put through a giant industrial **SHREDDER**.

The pet — hidden among 400 tons of waste — went through the factory's entire reprocessing system and amazingly emerged unscathed.

After being tipped on to a conveyor

**Flashback . . 1986 Sun**

*By ANDY RUSSELL*

belt he was **FED** into the blades of the huge mincer, which can rip apart fridges. He was then **DUMPED** into an enormous rotating drum before the machine **SPAT** him out the other side.

The rodent was eventually plucked from the final conveyor belt at the plant in Sandycroft, Flintshire. Miraculously he was alive — unlike the hamster eaten by comic Freddie Starr in 1986. Worker

Craig Bull, who took the pet home and gave it to his son Liam, ten, said yesterday: "It's beyond belief. He could have been killed at any stage in the process."

Craig has named the hamster Mike — after the colleague who found him. Workers have no idea how the pet got into the skip in the first place.

Craig's son Liam said in Gwernaffield, near Wrexham: "He's doing really well — although he looks a bit scruffy."

*a.russell@the-sun.co.uk*

The Guardian  Saturday June 3 2006

# The Great Hamster Escape (starring Mike)

Martin Wainwright

Another chapter was written yesterday in the history of great hamster escapes, when a pet called Mike survived three types of crushing machine and a shredder at a waste recycling plant.

The small rodent was left with only a minor foot injury after astonished staff discovered him limping into a final sorting area after going through a process which rips cookers and washing machines into stringy bits of metal.

Mike's white-knuckle ride through the Recyclo works on Deeside, north Wales, adds to the remarkable survival record of *Mesocricetus auratus* over many years. Hamsters have returned from premature burial, travelled through the post in envelopes (a highly illegal practice) and contentedly shared pet cages with poisonous snakes.

Mike's adventures rate highly in a sub-group of binmen sagas, particularly as Recyclo does not deal in food or similar rubbish which might attract pets.

'We don't get very much animal activity here,' said the plant's general manager, Tony Williams, who supervises some 400 tonnes a day of 'dry' waste. 'Some is shredded and then goes through the trammel – conveyor belts and grids which let the smaller pieces of waste fall through. It seems the hamster was small enough to pass through the 150mm gaps between the shredder blades, but big enough to pass along the trammel without dropping down.'

Hamsters are agile and energetic, regularly travelling up to eight miles during nocturnal hunts for food. Mike – named after one of the crew who found him – is thought to have gone a step too far in his explorations and ended up trapped in a Recyclo-bound white goods skip.

Unloaded at the plant, he was whirled in a rotating drum, taken on a conveyor to the shredder, bounced around in a giant sieve and then juddered along a moving grille whose waste disappears into sealed underground sumps. His survival of the four-minute process comfortably beats the waste-disposal record of Lucky, a hamster from the Anchorage Baptist temple in Alaska, who only had to deal with a municipal garbage truck.

The remotely familiar part of Mike's journey may have been the drum – a giant version of a hamster exercise ball. These have featured in other escapes: a hamster called Roly was found pedalling his along the hard shoulder of the M6 in Birmingham after falling from a car.

Pending possible calls from distraught owners, Mike is now getting to know Liam Bull, 10, whose father, Craig, was one of the rescue team. 'He's doing fine now,' said Liam. 'But I can't believe he's still alive after what happened to him.'

**White-knuckle ride**

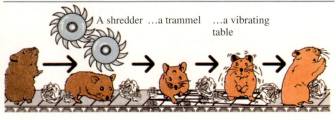

A shredder …a trammel …a vibrating table

When you plan any answer, you should spend no more than a few minutes identifying the key words in the question, and jotting down ideas in a logical way. This is how one student planned a paragraph on *content* (the first bullet point in the question on page 100).

Content

| Sun | Guardian |
| --- | --- |
| ❖ basic facts | ❖ detailed facts and background info |
| ❖ reference to another *Sun* story | ❖ reference to other hamster stories |
| ❖ quotations at end to give human interest | ❖ some quotations, but most from the plant manager – technical interest |

**13** Use the same method to plan a paragraph on *design* (the second bullet point in the question on page 100).

## Beginning your essay effectively

It is important to get your answer off to a good start. This will improve your chance of getting a good grade. Opening paragraphs should:

- ☑ show that you have understood the key words in the question
- ☑ give an overview of your approach
- ☑ not get stuck into too much detail.

**14** Read these three opening paragraphs and match them with the examiner's comments. Then put them in order of merit, with the best one first.

### Student 1

*In some ways the articles are very similar, for instance in the amount each gives to graphical features, but when you study them closely you realise that they are different in their impact on the reader.*

### Student 2

*In this answer I am going to compare two articles about a hamster. One is from the Guardian and the other is from the Sun. I shall write about the content, the design (including graphics) and the use of language.*

### Student 3

*The Guardian article leads you in with a cute colour photograph of a hamster. The Sun decides to focus on the graphic diagram of the hamster's journey, which it presents in black and white.*

### Examiner's comment a)

No attempt has been made to introduce the answer, although the comparison made is relevant and focused.

### Examiner's comment b)

This provides a good opening platform for developing an answer. The candidate is already making a comparison.

### Examiner's comment c)

This just repeats the question. A waste of valuable examination time!

**EXAM TIP**

The 'comparison' angle of this type of question lends itself to a plan in two columns. This allows you to collect features on both texts and compare them directly.

# Making an active comparison

When you compare two media texts, make your comparison as active as possible. This means:

- ☑ **directly comparing** the texts, not just listing the details in each one. Try to give a comment on each feature, showing its effect.

- ☑ **linking** the similarities/differences to the **audience** and **purpose** of each text

- ☑ taking into account the precise **focus of the question** when you compare

- ☑ covering **similarities** as well as **differences**, and all the bullet points.

---

**15** Read this extract from an A grade answer, which is discussing the way the texts present their material (the second bullet point in the question on page 100). Identify how the student has covered each of the points in the checklist above.

---

The Sun article is laid out on the page to make the hamster's journey as clear as possible. The subheading 'Pet takes terror trip...' couldn't be clearer, and it is put at the very top of the page. The diagram – carefully captioned with numbered steps – is the first thing the reader looks at. There is a similar diagram in the Guardian article, but it is squashed down at the foot of the page, probably because the text has already made the details of the journey clear enough. The layout entertains the readers in different ways too. The photo of the hamster in the Guardian is quite cute; the big headline in the Sun and the inset of the earlier Sun article emphasise humour. Each is entertaining in its own way.

---

**16** Read this extract from a D grade answer. It is comparing the use of language in the hamster texts. Rewrite it to improve its grade. Follow the checklist of points above, and use some of the techniques that you have just identified in the A grade answer above.

---

The Sun is the best description of the journey because it is so easy to read, like it uses lots of short words like SPAT. Though the first couple of sentences are quite long and use long words so there's a mixture. Some of the words are very descriptive like 'amazingly emerged unscathed', this shows the hamster came out all right. There's funny stuff as well, I think the headline has a pun. The other article also has some clever language, but the headline isn't as funny.

# Concluding the comparison

A successful conclusion to your comparison will:

☑ refer back to the key words in the question

☑ give an overview of your comparison

☑ refer to both texts but not go into detail or introduce a new point

☑ give your own view or evaluation.

> **17** Read the concluding paragraphs from two student essays below. Explain in detail why one of them is a grade A answer and one is grade D.

### Student 1

*Overall both articles are intended to amuse and inform the reader and both are successful in this respect. The Sun gives me a very clear idea from the graphics of what exactly happened to the hamster, whereas the Guardian gives a lot of entertaining background information. Its colour picture also acts as an attractive hook. The appeal of each depends on the individual – the Guardian provides lively reading and the Sun gives a vivid overview of the incident.*

### Student 2

*I think the Sun article is much better. I like the jokes and the pictures are really good. The Guardian article is very boring and there is too much to read, but I must admit I liked the picture – it looks just like my own hamster!*

> **18** Now use all the skills you have learnt in this unit to write a complete answer to the exam question on page 100.

**Remember** to:

- plan your answer carefully
- begin and end it effectively
- write an active comparison, commenting on the effect of the features, and taking audience and purpose into account.

## 4 Work with student answers

You are now going to pull together all the learning you have done in this section by attempting a complete answer. You will then study two other students' answers for comparison.

> **19 (a)** First read the leaflet on pages 106–107 and then answer the exam question on page 108. You have 40 minutes.
>
> **(b)** Then read the students' answers on pages 108–110 and the examiner comments.

## YOUR GUIDE TO BEACH SAFETY

Beach Lifeguards

Registered Charity No. 209603

BEACH SAFETY BEACH SAFETY BEACH SAFETY BEACH SAFETY BEACH SAFETY BEACH SAFETY BEACH SAFETY BEACH SAFETY BEACH SAFETY

### Know your flags
### What the different flags on the beach mean

Red and yellow flags mark areas of water that are patrolled by lifeguards. These are the safest places to swim.

When you see black and white chequered flags, it means an area of water has been marked for use by craft. For your own safety, do not swim in these zones.

The red flag indicates danger. Never enter the water when the red flag is flying.

An orange windsock flying at the beach indicates that wind conditions are especially dangerous – so under no circumstances should you take an inflatable into the sea.

**Remember:** never enter the water when you see a red flag flying.

For more information on beach safety, other safety literature or advice please call:

**0800 328 0600**

email
beachsafety@rnli.org.uk

or visit
www.rnli.org.uk/beachlifeguards

Beach Lifeguards

Photography: Myles New and Kirstin Prisk

The Royal National Lifeboat Institution
Registered Charity No. 209603

2004/10

# A fully integrated rescue service

RNLI lifeboats provide on call, the 24-hour service necessary to cover search and rescue requirements up to 50 miles out from the coast of the United Kingdom and the Republic of Ireland. There are 231 lifeboat stations.

The RNLI lifeguard service operates on beaches throughout the south west of England. The lifeguard service brings together best practices from around the world ensuring the service standards are the highest possible.

The RNLI depends on voluntary contributions and legacies for its income.

# How you can help save lives

Please, make a gift to help support the RNLI, so we can continue to train and equip more lifeguards and lifeboat crews. Only with your support can we ensure they can be there to help someone in difficulty – perhaps even someone you know.

**Your gift will help the RNLI save more lives.**

To make a donation call our hotline on **0800 543210** or to donate online **www.rnli.org.uk/beachlifeguards**

RNLI lifeguards work along side *Lifesavers* – the Royal Life Saving Society UK and the Surf Life Saving Association of GB

## To stay safe, remember F.L.A.G.S. whenever you are at the beach:

**F** — **Find the red and yellow flags and swim between them.**
Always swim where there is a lifeguard on patrol, and stay inside the area marked by the red and yellow flags. Never swim where a sign says not to, or when the red flag is flying.

**L** — **Look at the safety signs.**
Always read and obey the safety signs – they will help you avoid potential dangers on the beach, and to identify the safest areas for swimming.

**A** — **Ask a Lifeguard for advice.**
If in doubt, it's always best to play it safe and ask the experts.

**G** — **Get a friend to swim with you.**
Make sure there are other people around, because you never know when help might be needed.

**S** — **Stick your hand in the air and shout for help if you get into difficulty.**

If you see someone in difficulty, tell a lifeguard. If you can't see a lifeguard call 999 and ask for the Coastguard.

# It's a great day to be at the beach

The UK and the Republic of Ireland are lucky enough to have some of the finest, cleanest beaches. Mile upon mile of golden sand, clean water and lots of summer attractions.

That's why many people enjoy our beaches every year – for day trips, family holidays, swimming, surfing and more.

## RNLI makes the beach a safer place

Every year thousands of people get into real, life-threatening difficulty. They may be washed out to sea, pulled under by a strong rip current, or simply get into the water when the conditions are dangerous.

Last year in the UK, around 70 people drowned off Britain's beaches. We don't want that to happen to you or to someone you love.

It's also why we've compiled some simple steps you can take to stay safe on the beach.

How does the leaflet 'Your Guide to Beach Safety' produced by The Royal National Lifeboat Institution (RNLI) encourage the reader to think about safety at the beach and the work of lifeguards and lifeboats?

You should comment on the following:
- the information given in the leaflet
- the use of language
- headings
- design features, including layout, use of colour, photographs and pictures
- any other aspects which you think are relevant.

## Student 1

A clear introduction, which shows the student has understood the question. How could the answer be improved by developing the last sentence slightly?

Some reasonable but very vague points.

Compare this with the 2nd paragraph of Student 2's response. What makes that one better?

The student uses Point – Evidence – Comment quite well when analysing 'emotive language'. Improve the sentence about 'short and punchy' language by adding a comment on its effect.

Too much description and too much on colours, but the student tries to relate points to the question. Which bullet point from the question has the student **not** covered?

Quite a good conclusion. How is Student 2's conclusion even more effective? Think about (a) the content, (b) the style of the answer.

This leaflet is designed to encourage beach users to think about safety and the work of the lifeguards. It does this by using a number of techniques.

There is a lot of information given in this leaflet and it is all over the page, the information mainly concerns safety but there are also some other areas. There is information on how the reader can help to save lives by giving to the RNLI, there is a donations section in the corner. There is information on how to be safe as well, this shows the various flags and what they mean and what to do. This all emphasises safety. It also includes a telephone number and website to find out more.

The language used in the leaflet also reminds the reader to be safe. It does this by using emotive language for example 'Last year in the U.K. around 70 people drowned off Britain's beaches. We don't want that to happen to you or to someone you love.' This gives a bad scenario and puts you in that situation, by talking directly to you. It repeats the words 'Beach Safety' at the top of the page to get visitors to associate beach with safety. A lot of the language in the text is also short and punchy for instance 'never enter the water when you see a red flag flying'. All the writing in the leaflet is useful whether it's about how to raise money or how to encourage the use of the lifeguards. There is also positive language to give you a break from the information, 'Mile upon mile of golden sand, clean water and lots of summer attractions.'

The design features in this leaflet are good because there are a lot of photos and a lot of colour, mainly red and yellow, this is because these colours represent the colours of the Lifeguards, it reminds us to think of them and stay safe. Another reason there is a lot of red is to remind us of the red flag, this is the danger flag and we are reminded about it throughout the leaflet. Blue is another colour that is used, this links to the sea and summer skies. There are a lot of action pictures of lifeguards doing their jobs and helping. These show they are on the alert all the time and are well equipped but it also shows how dangerous the beach can be and that we must always think of safety.

In conclusion I think that the leaflet encourages the reader to be safe very well, because it is bright and informative. I think this leaflet will get noticed a lot because it is bright. It is probably targeted for adults to read and then tell their children. It will always get a reaction no matter who sees it.

1

5

10

15

20

25

30

35

# The examiner's view

This answer makes several useful points about language and layout, and it supports its ideas with quotations. The answer is very well organised as each paragraph has a different topic which relates to a bullet point in the question. The answer could be improved by making the points more focused, by commenting more and describing less, by reducing the repetition and by covering all the bullet points in the question.

**A grade C**

**20** Assess your own answer against this C grade answer. Look at the 'Steps to success in reading' on page 7 to check how well you are meeting the assessment objectives. What do you need to work on to improve your grade?

## Student 2

Information leaflets are everywhere. The task of the writer and designer is to combine their talents so that the reader is encouraged to pick up the leaflet, then continue to absorb the information and advice. The RNLI leaflet manages to do this.

At first glance the leaflet is packed full of information of all kinds, apparently scattered over the pages. However, it is actually quite carefully organised, as each page is devoted to a different topic. There is a page with some information about beaches, for example, followed by a page with advice on how to be safe while on the beach. Two other pages cover the lifeguards flags and the work of the RNLI. It is important for a reader not to be confused or put off when they read a safety leaflet like this, so the careful organisation encourages them to read on. The information is even carefully organised within each page. The best example of this is 'It's a great day to be at the beach'. The first half gives the reader some positive facts about beaches; the second half then gives the other side of the story: the dangers. This effectively leads the reader on to the advice page.

The leaflet's use of language is also designed to keep the reader's attention. The passages of information are written in very clear, straightforward language, for example 'Last year in the UK about 70 people drowned off Britain's beaches.' No fuss, no nonsense. The sentences are often short, again for this purpose, although the sentence against the orange windsock would be better divided into two. The advice text uses the technique of direct address; each piece of advice begins with a command, for example 'Look at the safety signs'. This helps to get the reader's attention, and remind them that it could be YOU who is in need of these tips. The use of a mnemonic (FLAGS) is another clever way of encouraging the reader to take note, as it makes the job of remembering easier.

The headings on the leaflet have a huge impact because they are the first things that the reader will look at. They are all in red and/or blue, which helps to give the design some unity. There is a variety of styles in the headings: some are white letters on a red background, for example. Variety is another way of keeping the reader's interest.

The student always has the reader of the leaflet in mind in the answer. Find two examples of this.

This is a well developed example. Explain how the student uses PEC to analyse how the leaflet is 'carefully organised'.

The student is not afraid of criticising the leaflet. Find an example of such criticism. Is it backed up with evidence and reasons?

The two main design features of the leaflet are the photographs and the use of colour. Some of the photos are action shots, to give the leaflet interest; others show lifeguards with binoculars, which reminds us of what the lifeguards do. The predominant colours relate to three aspects of the subject matter: the sea (blue), lifeguards (yellow) and danger (red). The way that the designer has arranged FLAGS with the white letter on a red flag, and going vertically instead of horizontally, helps to make the letter stand out. Each is the start of a sentence of advice and the device helps the reader to remember it. A repeated slogan BEACH SAFETY runs across the top of the leaflet, reminding us of the link between the two.

This leaflet encourages the reader to think about safety by enticing him in with clear and intelligent design, then presenting the information effectively. It manages to give us a lot of information about the lifeboat service and lifeguards alongside the safety tips. Colour, design and text and photography all combine to do their job.

## The examiner's view

The answer makes perceptive points about language and layout, and there are good ideas on all the bullet points. It is expressed clearly and fluently, and the answer is well organised. The student has avoided a 'run of the mill' introduction and conclusion, shows an independent view and uses the correct technical terms where appropriate.

**A grade A**

**21** Assess your own answer against this grade A answer. Look at the 'Steps to success in reading' on page 7 to check how well you are meeting the assessment objectives. What do you need to work on to improve your grade?

# F  Reading non-fiction texts (unseen)

By the end of this section you will have sharpened three key skills that are important to improve your answer on non-fiction texts (unseen):

1 understand key features of different kinds of non-fiction

2 read and understand a text in timed conditions

3 comment on the writer's use of language and other key features

You will also assess your skills through answering questions about non-fiction texts, similar to the ones you will meet in the exam. You will then explore the qualities of answers at different grades.

**IN THE EXAM**
**SPECIFICATION B ONLY**

- There is one question, which is based on one extract.
- The first time you see the extract will be in the exam.
- The extract is about 650 words long.
- This question is worth 10% of your total mark for GCSE English.
- You must answer the question in 40 minutes.
- Your answer to this question will be assessed against Reading assessment objectives (i), (iv) and (v). See page 6.

## Reading non-fiction texts

'Non-fiction' refers to texts that are based on real life and facts. Non-fiction texts are not imagined or made up. They include feature articles from newspapers, magazines and the internet, information books, biographies, autobiographies and travel writing.

Examples of non-fiction texts can be found on pages 47–66 of the Edexcel Anthology.

## What is the examiner looking for?

Below are the characteristics of a good answer and of a weak answer. Find the pairs of comments that match. This activity will focus your attention on the qualities that will gain you marks in this section of the exam. The first one has been done for you.

| A good answer | A weak answer |
|---|---|
| • focuses on what the question is asking about the non-fiction text | • summarises the non-fiction text with little reference to the question |

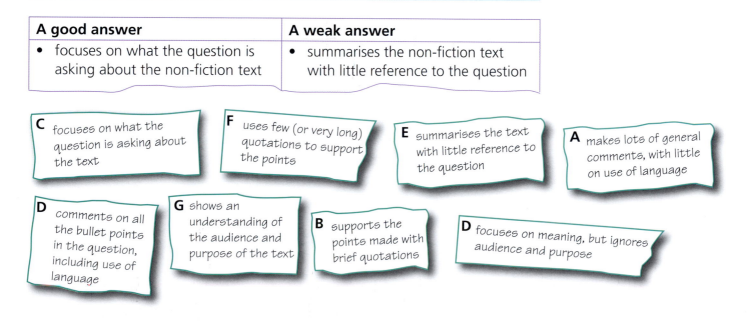

**C** focuses on what the question is asking about the text

**F** uses few (or very long) quotations to support the points

**E** summarises the text with little reference to the question

**A** makes lots of general comments, with little on use of language

**D** comments on all the bullet points in the question, including use of language

**G** shows an understanding of the audience and purpose of the text

**B** supports the points made with brief quotations

**D** focuses on meaning, but ignores audience and purpose

## 1 Understand key features of different kinds of non-fiction

You could be given any kind of non-fiction text in the exam. To answer the question well, it is important to recognise the kind of text you have been given. Examiners will expect you to show an understanding of:

☑ the kind of non-fiction text it is and therefore the features it displays

☑ the purpose of the text

☑ its audience

☑ the language features used

☑ how it is organised (its structure).

## Different kinds of non-fiction

**Different kinds of non-fiction**

- Information text
- Autobiography
- Feature article
- Biography
- Travel writing.

**1** Read the extracts from five different types of non-fiction text below. Match each one up with a kind of non-fiction from the list in the margin.

**A**

- Why is it written in present tense?
- What do you notice about the lengths of the sentences?

The Spitfire shudders as each of eight guns pours out 1,200 rounds a minute.

Almost at once somebody in that 88 sees me. He goes into a steepish turn away, turning back out to sea. I follow, firing short bursts at him the whole time, spraying lead all over the sky. If only I could see just that little bit more. Easing in astern of him I am quite close and flying automatically. I'm sure I can see hits; hope it's not imagination. There is no return fire as he eases out of his turn and pulls up towards the cloud base.

**B**

- This is descriptive writing – comment on the effectiveness of the adjectives used.

My grandmother Jenny Fulcher grew up in the East End. To be an East Ender then was to be among the lowest of London's poor, but she never thought of herself as low. To Jenny, there was only respectable and common and by her own account she was respectable. This had nothing to do with money – no one in the East End had much of that; it had to do with blood and conduct.

Jenny was salty and wilful, as thin and prickly as the reeds that once grew where she was born.

**C**

Looking back, the biggest culture shock about Japan was not the chopsticks or the raw octopus, it was the shock of discovering that no matter where you go you instantly become the topic of conversation. At first it's an ego boost. You feel like a celebrity. 'Sorry, no autographs today, I'm in a hurry.' But you soon realise that in Japan foreigners are not so much celebrities as they are objects of curiosity and entertainment. It is a stressful situation, and it has broken better men than me.

Can you see where the following techniques are used?

– exaggeration
– contrast
– short and long sentences
– humour

**D**

Planning a holiday with a teenager is like no ot0her holiday experience. Many teenagers blithely announce they don't want to go on holiday with you at all and would rather hang out at home with their friends.

Letting them stay alone at home even at the age of 16 or 17, however, is never a good idea: it's too much responsibility for them, and will prevent you from enjoying your holiday.

Is this extract largely fact or opinion?

**E**

A number of Victorians were terrified of being buried alive. Wilkie Collins, who wrote two of the first and most famous thrillers – *The Moonstone* and *The Woman in White* – left instructions for various tests to be made before he was buried, so that there should be no doubt that he was dead. A Russian, Count Karnicki, invented a coffin with a glass ball resting on top of the body. If the corpse moved, the ball released a spring and the lid would fly open.

Notice how a general point is supported by explanation and examples. Which sentence makes the general point?

# Audience and purpose

You cannot comment properly on the text you are given without thinking about its audience and purpose.

> **2** Draw up a table like the one below and match the audiences and purposes listed below to the types of non-fiction. One line has been filled in as an example.

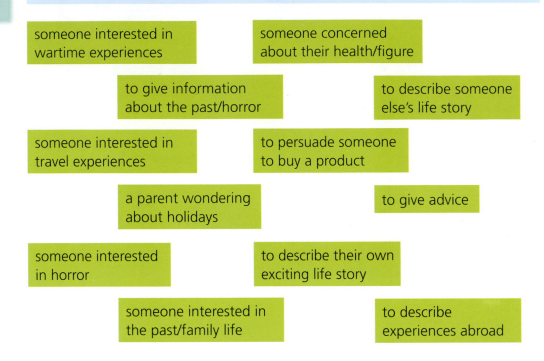

someone interested in wartime experiences

someone concerned about their health/figure

to give information about the past/horror

to describe someone else's life story

someone interested in travel experiences

to persuade someone to buy a product

a parent wondering about holidays

to give advice

someone interested in horror

to describe their own exciting life story

someone interested in the past/family life

to describe experiences abroad

| Kind of non-fiction | Purpose | Audience |
|---|---|---|
| Autobiography | to describe their own exciting life story | someone interested in wartime experiences |
| Information text | | |
| Feature article | | |
| Travel writing | | |
| Biography | | |

To get a good grade in this section of the exam you should:

☑ understand what the question is asking of you

☑ sharpen your reading skills so that you can actively read and understand the text in the context of the question

☑ use the information in the question to plan your answer.

## Understanding the question

Exam questions about non-fiction texts will always start with a **leading sentence**. This often begins 'How…?' or 'In what ways…?'. It focuses on the **purpose** of the passage and asks you to comment on how this is put across to the **audience**. For example:

How does this passage make the subject of space exploration interesting for the ordinary reader?

This asks you about the methods of the writer – you need to think about purpose of the text

This asks you to think about the audience

This gives a focus for your discussion

3  For each of the sentences from exam questions in the table below, pick out the key words you should be thinking about as you read the text. The first one has been done for you.

| Non-fiction text | Leading sentence in exam question |
|---|---|
| Information text | How does this passage make the subject of space exploration interesting for the ordinary reader? |
| Autobiography | How does the writer create a vivid impression of his experiences in this passage? |
| Biography | In what ways does the passage bring out the strengths and weaknesses of the central character? |
| Travel writing | How does the writer convey the special excitement of travel? |
| Newspaper or magazine article | In what ways does this article make its subject entertaining for teenagers? |

4  Read the exam question below, then test yourself on how quickly you can read and understand the article which is at the top of page 116. Time how long it takes you.

In what ways does the writer of this article show that she understands the needs and worries of parents?

Planning a holiday with a teenager is like no other holiday experience. Many teenagers blithely announce they don't want to go on holiday with you at all and would rather hang out at home with their friends.

Letting them stay alone at home even at the age of 16 or 17, however, is never a good idea: it's too much responsibility for them, and will prevent you from enjoying your holiday.

Most parents are unwilling to have their home turned into a rave for two weeks, so the art of persuading a teenager to go on holiday with you takes stealth and cunning.

On the plus side, holidays can be a great time for bringing parents and teenagers together. Away from domestic and academic demands, this is a wonderful time to talk and do things as a family. You won't have them at home for much longer, so make the most of it.

How long did you take? If you read it in about a minute, you are doing well! Note that this passage is about a quarter of the length of the text that you will face in the exam.

5 Read the openings of these two student answers to the question at the bottom of page 115.

(a) Which one has understood the question and is on the way to getting a good grade? Give your reasons.

(b) What advice would you give to the other student to boost the answer's grade?

**Student 1**

Like many good writers of advice, this writer really knows how to address her readers' fears and worries. The content, language and organisation of her advice are judged just right.

Right from the start she shows that she is aware how difficult holidays with teenagers can be, by …

**Student 2**

I don't think this writer can ever have had a teenager in her family! Or if she did, then they weren't proper teenagers at all, but meekly followed whatever orders the parents dealt out. You really can't force teenagers to go on holiday with you. The reasons she gives are all feeble, as I intend to show.

First, teenagers are quite capable of looking after their parents' house...

# Using the bullet points

The leading sentence in the exam question is always followed by some bullet points. These list the topics that you should cover in your answer. One bullet will always be on the way the writer has used language, such as their choice of words, the way they put their sentences together, and the tone of the writing.

**6** Read the question below and pick out the key words. Then study the piece of travel writing underneath carefully.

> In the following extract, Sarah Biles describes a hot and dusty bus journey in East Africa.
>
> How does the writer give the reader a vivid impression of an uncomfortable journey in Africa in this passage?
>
> You should write about
> ❖ the conditions in the bus
> ❖ the use of language, especially words that appeal to our senses
> ❖ the people, animals and things
> ❖ the effect the journey has on the writer.

Imagine a small minibus, you know the sort, one that would hold about fifteen people comfortably. Now imagine that number of people tripled; three conductors (I have still not been able to work out why); a live goat squeezed into the boot, bleating helplessly; tranquil chickens lying quietly under the seats, their legs tied together; a Masai tribesman, with his huge spear, dangerously squashed in; assortments of baskets and containers, carrying anything from bananas to the locally-made potent brew of mbege,[1] packed into the aisles and racks overhead.

The pungent smell of fermenting mixes with the body odours of the slowly cooking bodies and the fumes from the ancient bus. Bob Marley blasts from the radio as the driver crunches the gears and babies start crying. On the roof the frame and cushions of a new sofa are strapped on precariously.

The bus stops to pick us up. We cram into a three millimetre square area and thank God that we are only going a short way. The bus proceeds down the mountain, swaying, lurching and braking as we avoid the pot holes, mud slides and other buses which are dodging from either side of the road to find the smoothest ride.

Further down the slope there has been no rain, and the choking dust comes drifting in through cracks in the windows and holes in the floor. Some people cover themselves but I cannot move, so dust mixes with sweat and soon I have dirty red streaks down my face.

([1]mbege is alcohol)

**7** Two students have started to make notes for their answers. Student 1's notes are on the first bullet point. Student 2's notes are on the second bullet point.

**(a)** What makes Student 2's notes better than Student 1's? Think about:
- how relevant they are
- the number of points that are made
- whether and how they are linked to the text.

**(b)** Improve Student 1's notes so that the answer will get a higher grade. If you have time, make your own notes on the third and fourth bullet points.

## EXAM TIP

You have 40 minutes to answer the question. You should spend up to 10 minutes of this time:

1. reading and understanding the question
2. reading the text with the question in mind
3. planning your answer by making notes on the bullet points, for example, by highlighting or underlining relevant sentences, or by annotating in the margin of the text. You can also use the bullet points to organise your answer, for example with one paragraph for each point.

### Student 1
Conditions
– small bus
– ?is it real or imagined?
– no rain – v. dry conditions

### Student 2
Language
– Words suggesting being crowded
– Words suggesting noises
– Words suggesting smells
– Overall: lots of details and images
– humour (exaggeration – 3mm square area)
– addressing reader (you know) – intimacy, direct

**Remember** that to comment effectively you need to:

- **Make a range of different points.** Develop the points by going into more detail. Use quotations and refer to the text.

- **Show that you understand the features.** Refer to their purpose and how they create an effect for the reader.

- **Link the points together.** Use connecting words and phrases such as 'however, 'also', 'another technique'.

- **Evaluate the passage overall.** Give your balanced opinion in a final paragraph.

The bullet points in the exam question help you to **identify** the key features of the text. But to improve the grade of your answer you have to do more than this. You need to **comment** on these features.

In this unit we will be focusing on boosting your grade in three areas – when you comment on language, organisation and tone/viewpoint.

## Commenting on language

In the passage below Geoffrey Wellum, a Royal Air Force pilot in World War II, describes his experience of flying a Spitfire fighter over the sea near England. He is hunting an invading plane, a Junkers 88, which is attacking ships.

> **8** Read the passage, keeping in mind the exam question below. Remember to read the passage actively, thinking about why the writer has used words and sentences in the way he has.

How does the writer's use of language help the reader share his experience of flying a fighter plane in battle?

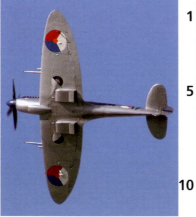

1  I close, tense and trembling a little. I want to be sick. Why after my experiences do I continue to feel so? Some sort of strain? The weather? Don't know, but I should be thoroughly ashamed of myself. Have a go, Geoff, don't waste time or he will see you and pop back into cloud like a dose of salts.[1] Closing, a little closer, Geoff,
5  and still I don't think he has seen me. Astonishing. Must be looking for ships. I've calmed down. Lay off deflection[2] … just a shade … not too much. He's no more than a blurred image through the rainy oily windscreen. Draw the bead[3] through the line of light … that's about it. Press the button. The Spitfire shudders as each of eight guns pours out 1,200 rounds a minute.

10    Almost at once somebody in that 88 sees me. He goes into a steepish turn away, turning back out to sea. I follow, firing short bursts at him the whole time, spraying lead all over the sky. If only I could see just that little bit more. Easing in astern[4] of him I am quite close and flying automatically. I'm sure I can see hits; hope it's not imagination. There is no return fire as he eases out of his turn and pulls up towards the cloud base. Only time now for a quick snap shot … a fraction of a second. Very
15  close, my fire must be reasonably accurate. Too late, he pulls up into cloud and disappears. That's that.

---

[1] This means 'very quickly'; 'salts' refers to an old fashioned medicine
[2] A flying term, which probably means 'stop turning a bit'
[3] Another technical term; this is part of the gun sight (used for aiming)
[4] This means 'behind him'

**9** Now read this A grade answer and answer the questions in the boxes. They get you to analyse how well the student has commented on the language of the passage.

> The writer uses the pronoun 'I', which gives a strong sense of personal experience. The fact that the whole passage is written in the present tense also makes it feel more immediate, as though everything is happening as I am reading it. For example, 'I want to be sick' – this is what he is feeling right now, in the plane. A similar technique is the writer's use of very short sentences, for instance 'The weather?' He is trying to show the kind of thoughts that were occurring to him at the time – in short bursts. The short sentences also indicate the speed with which things are happening. The author uses sentence structure very well, because he also uses ellipses (...) to suggest the tense pauses before something happens suddenly. With 'Lay off deflection ... just a shade' you can almost see him adjusting the controls.
>
> Another technique that the writer uses is to show his anxiety. He talks to himself ('Geoff, don't waste time') and shares his fears. It must have been terrifying flying in a combat plane, and this comes across to the reader.
>
> The writing is made more convincing by the use of technical terms such as 'easing in astern'. These terms add to the realism; it makes the experience more authentic. Overall the passage reads like a radio commentary or voice over, so you feel as if you are listening to events as they are happening.

The student makes a range of points in the first paragraph. What are they?

The student gives an **example** here to back up the point being made. Find another example of this.

This phrase helps to **connect** the points. What other connecting words and phrases does the student use?

The student shows an understanding of the **purpose** and **effect** of the language features. Which sentence in this paragraph shows this?

The student gives an **overview** in the last sentence, but could boost the answer's grade still further by giving a personal **evaluation**. Add this yourself.

Has the answer focused on the question throughout?

**10** Now answer this question on the passage about the bus journey in East Africa (page 117 above). You can build on the notes that Student 2 has already made (page 117).

> How does the writer use language to give the reader a vivid impression of an uncomfortable journey in Africa in this passage?

*Remember* that a high grade answer will:
- always focus on the question
- make a range of different points
- use quotations and textual references
- show that you understand the purpose and effect of the language features
- link the points
- provide an evaluation in the final sentence.

## EXAM TIP

Using technical terms in your answer, such as 'ellipsis' and 'jargon', can help to convince the examiner that you really know what you are writing about. If you can't remember the right term, use your own words. You could use 'technical words' instead of 'jargon' and 'a row of dots to show a pause' instead of 'ellipsis.'

# Commenting on organisation

Sometimes the exam question will ask you to comment on the organisation of the passage. You should focus on these features:

☑ Has the writer used **paragraphs** to organise the different points being made? Are the paragraphs varied in length for effect?

☑ Is there a variety of **sentence structure**? How is **punctuation** used to break up long sentences?

☑ Does the **order** of the material have a particular purpose? Are any **linking phrases** or **signpost** words and phrases used to guide the reader through the text?

When you comment on these features, remember to make a range of points and quote evidence from the text.

> **11** Look at the following examination question, and read the passage below. Melanie McGrath is writing about her grandmother, Jenny, who lived in the East End of London at the start of the last century.

> How does the writer present a vivid impression of her grandmother?
>
> You should write about
> ❖ key features of her character
> ❖ the way the details are organised
> ❖ the use of language.

1   My grandmother Jenny Fulcher grew up in the East End. To be an East Ender then was to be among the lowest of London's poor, but she never thought of herself as low. To Jenny, there was only respectable and common and by her own account she was respectable. This had nothing
5   to do with money – no one in the East End had much of that; it had to do with blood[1] and conduct.
    Jenny was salty and wilful, as thin and prickly as the reeds that once grew where she was born. Her heart was full of tiny thorns, which chafed but were never big enough to make her bleed. Vague feelings
10   drifted about her like mist: bitterness, resentment and rage, mostly. Life was as much a mystery to her as she was to herself. She'd spend hours plotting how to squeeze an extra rasher of bacon from the butcher, but on the bigger issues she was helpless. She grasped the details without understanding anything of the general rules. She never had the means to
15   manage her life and so was destined to be bent in the shape of desires, urges and ambitions greater than her own.
    All the same, when her face lit up it was like a door swinging out into sunshine. There was something irrepressibly naughty about her. You'd imagine her standing behind your back poking her tongue out at you. She
20   revelled in playing the martyr[2] but was comically bad at the part. She'd insist on giving you the last piece of cake, then reach into her handbag when she thought you weren't looking, pull out a huge bar of chocolate, stuff it in her mouth all at once and pretend she had a cough and couldn't

talk. Her luxuriant moaning had to be witnessed to be believed. On bad
25  days everything from her kidneys to her knitting cost too much, ached like
Geronimo³ or was doing its best to rip her off.

No life is without its joys, though, and Jenny harboured two great
passions. The first of these was the crystallised juice of an Indian grass,
otherwise known as sugar. She spooned it into her tea in extravagant
30  quantities and whenever she thought no one was looking, she'd lick a
bony finger, dunk it in the sugar bowl and jam it into her mouth. She was
partial to biscuits, cakes, marmalade, tarts and chocolate too, but sweets
were really her thing. Though she didn't realise it, my grandmother's
other great love was the East End. She moaned about it constantly – the
35  cramped streets with their potholed pavements, the filthy kids and the
belching factories – but she hated the thought of leaving, even for a day.

---

¹ blood here means family   ² playing the martyr means pretending to be very unlucky or a victim
³ like Geronimo – we would say 'ached like mad'. This was presumably one of Jenny's expressions.

**12** Now read these extracts from two students' responses. They are focusing
on the second bullet point in the question – 'the way the details are
organised' – which refers to the structure of the piece.

Evaluate each response by checking it against the list of features above
(page 120) and thinking how well the students comment on these
features. Which would be awarded a high grade, and which would not?
Give your reasons.

## Student 1

McGrath organises her material well, so that the picture of her grandmother
is presented carefully and with full effect. She begins by referring to the
East End – this is an essential background, which explains much of Jenny's
character. When she returns to this theme at the end of the passage she
is emphasising that theme, as well as drawing the threads together in a
satisfying way for the reader.

She uses the short sentence to draw attention to an important point. For
example: 'There was something irrepressibly naughty about her' makes a
general point which is then followed by an example.

Each paragraph of the passage covers a different aspect of Jenny's
character, for example the second one describes the difficult feelings that
she had. And when McGrath moves on in the third paragraph to explore the
other side of Jenny's character, she signals this clearly with 'All the same...'

## Student 2

The writer talks about lots of things in this passage, but all of them are
about Jenny, who is her grandmother. She begins by saying she comes
from the East End, which is in London, then she describes her anger and
bitterness: 'Vague feelings drifted about her like mist: bitterness, resentment
and rage, mostly'. She could be naughty too, which made her happy. She liked
sugar and the East End – an odd mix of things to end.

# Commenting on tone and viewpoint

**Tone** refers to the atmosphere created by the writer's language and expression. It is a bit like the 'mood' of the piece. Some common tones are:

❖ **formal** and **serious**, with long sentences and careful attention to the rules of standard English

❖ **informal** and **light-hearted**, with humour and some casual expressions

❖ **emotive**, with lots of powerful words and an appeal to the reader's feelings.

**Viewpoint** is the position (or perspective) from which the writer approaches the subject matter of the text:

❖ A **personal** viewpoint often uses 'I' (1st person) or 'you' (2nd person) to engage with the reader.

❖ An **impersonal** viewpoint uses the 3rd person ('he', 'she', 'it', 'they').

The writer's **role** is another aspect to consider. Is the writer a participant, a critic, an observer, a parent, a consumer…? How does this affect the choice of language used?

> **13** Practise spotting tone and viewpoint in the extracts in this section. Copy and complete the table below. Give a quotation in each case to back up your decision about tone.

| Extract | Tone | Viewpoint |
|---|---|---|
| Planning a holiday with a teenager (page 116) | formal and understanding, but with a light touch<br><br>e.g. '… takes stealth and cunning' | |
| Imagine a small minibus (page 117) | | 1st person – a traveller |
| I close, tense and trembling (page 118) | | |
| My grandmother Jenny Fulcher (page 120) | | |

> **14** Read the exam question and extract opposite. The three student responses (page 124) cover the first bullet point – analysing the tone of the piece. Match the responses with the examiners' comments.

In the following extract, the writer guides tourists on what they might want to see or do in London.

How does this guide book entry use language to present advice and information in a useful and entertaining way?

You should write about
❖ the tone used by the writer
❖ the viewpoint of the writer
❖ the use of language.

# LONDON DUNGEON

Blood! Gore! Disease! At the London Dungeon, you'll experience the thrill of disgust at the true horror London can offer. And that's only the length of the queue. Seriously, if you want to join the other screamers at this delightfully camped-up gorefest, it's a good idea to buy tickets online beforehand. Otherwise, you're generally looking at a tortured hour or more standing in line.

The ridiculously popular dungeon is basically a souped-up house of horrors, where you walk and are transported by fairground-ride boat through a landscape of London's gruesome history. Here you can watch people die of plague or hang on the Tyburn gallows, listen to Anne Boleyn before her head was deftly separated from her shoulders, and wonder at the assortment of ingenious methods of torture.

By the time Judgment Day arrives, you'll find yourself condemned to death and put aboard the executioner's barge for a 'final trip' through Traitors' Gate. At the Great Fire of London exhibit, you'll run – literally – through a gauntlet of flames.

As a spectator, it's nice to see that you're keeping all those actors in steady jobs.

## Student 1

The writer of the guide book cleverly uses a mixture of tones to deliver his information and advice. First of all there is a lot of drama, such as in the opening three words, each with an exclamation mark. This emphasises the dramatic nature of the London Dungeon. Almost immediately, however, he undercuts this by showing humour ('And that's only the length of the queue'). The humour often has the effect of puncturing the importance of the scene, for example when he points out at the end that the dungeon is full of actors who need to keep their jobs. Finally, he also adopts the helpful tone of someone giving advice, such as 'Seriously ... it's a good idea...' Overall, the tone changes so fast in this short piece that the reader has difficulty knowing what its true purpose is.

## Student 2

The tone is pretty informal as the writer uses words like 'gorefest' and 'souped-up'. This is because he wants to get on the reader's side, he wants them to like him. I don't really like his tone as its too shouty – all those exclamation marks at the beginning are like someone calling you to a circus. He takes the mickey like calling the dungeon ridiculously popular, if he doesn't like it, why doesn't he just stay away?

## Student 3

Some parts of this piece are advice to the traveller so they are in an advice style, like 'Seriously, if you want to join...' This is because he is advising you when to get tickets. The tone is also very 'emotive' as lots of emotive words are used to get your feelings going like 'thrill of disgust'. He wants to make you frightened to show that the dungeon is a frightening place. Although he laughs at it as well.

### Examiner's comment a)

The student begins well by identifying an important aspect of the tone of the piece, but misunderstands the author's purpose. The language is also too casual in places.
**Grade D**

### Examiner's comment b)

Some excellent points, all relevant to the tone. The points are developed with brief but good references to the text, and the use of connectives makes the student's writing fluent. A well-argued personal opinion ends the evaluation.
**Grade A\***

### Examiner's comment c)

The student makes several points, and has attempted to develop two of them, with varying levels of success. Relevant quotations from the text are used. The answer could be improved by developing the point about humour, which is important.
**Grade C**

15 Now write a paragraph focusing on the second bullet point of the question on page 123 (commenting on the writer's viewpoint). Remember that a high grade answer will:
  ■ make a range of different points
  ■ use quotations and textual references
  ■ show that you understand the purpose and effect of the viewpoint
  ■ link the points
  ■ provide an evaluation in the final sentence.

## 4 Work with student answers

You are now going to pull together all the learning you have done in this section by attempting a complete answer. You will then study two other student's answers for comparison.

**16 (a)** First read the exam question and the passage below, and answer the question. You have 40 minutes.

**(b)** Then read the students' answers and examiner's comments on pages 126–128 and complete the activites in the boxes by each answer.

---

Read the extract from George Alagiah's book *A Passage to Africa*. How does this passage bring out the challenges faced by the writer as a television journalist reporting scenes of suffering?

You should write about:
- ❖ the kinds of stories and pictures needed for television
- ❖ the physical and emotional demands of his work
- ❖ the thoughts and feelings caused by the man's smile
- ❖ the use of language.

Support your answer with examples from the text.

---

*George Alagiah writes about his experiences as a television reporter during the war in Somalia, Africa in the 1990s. He won a special award for his report on the incidents described in this passage.*

I saw a thousand hungry, lean, scared and betrayed faces as I crisscrossed Somalia between the end of 1991 and December 1992, but there is one I will never forget. I was in a little hamlet just outside Gufgaduud, a village in the back of beyond, a place the aid agencies had yet to reach.

In the ghoulish manner of journalists on the hunt for the most striking pictures, my cameraman and I tramped from one hut to another. What might have appalled us when we'd started our trip just a few days before no longer impressed us much. The search for the shocking is like the craving for a drug: you require heavier and more frequent doses the longer you're at it. Pictures that stun the editors one day are written off as the same old stuff the next. This sounds callous, but it is just a fact of life. It's how we collect and compile the images that so move people in the comfort of their sitting rooms back home.

There was Amina Abdirahman, who had gone out that morning in search of wild, edible roots, leaving her two young girls lying on the dirt floor of their hut. They had been sick for days, and were reaching the final stages of hunger. Habiba was ten years old and her sister, Ayaan, was nine. By the time Amina returned, she had only one daughter. Habiba had died. No rage, no whimpering, just a passing away. It was, as I said at the time in my dispatch, a vision of 'famine away from the headlines, a famine of quiet suffering and lonely death'.

There was the old woman who lay in her hut, abandoned by relations who were too weak to carry her on their journey to find food. It was the smell that drew me to her doorway: the smell of decaying flesh. Where her shinbone should have been there was a festering wound the size of my hand. She'd been shot in the leg as the retreating army of the deposed dictator took revenge on whoever it found in its way.

And, then there was the face I will never forget.

I saw that face for only a few seconds, a fleeting meeting of eyes before the face turned away, as its owner retreated into the darkness of another hut. In those brief moments there had been a smile, not from me, but from the face. It was not a smile of greeting, it was not a smile of joy – how could it be? – but it was a smile nonetheless. It touched me in a way I could not explain. It moved me in a way that went beyond pity or revulsion.[1]

What was it about that smile? I had to find out. I urged my translator to ask the man why he had smiled. He came back with an answer. 'It's just that he was embarrassed to be found in this condition,' the translator explained. And then it clicked. That's what the smile had been about. It was the feeble smile that goes with apology, the kind of smile you might give if you felt you had done something wrong.

Normally inured² to stories of suffering, accustomed to the evidence of deprivation, I was unsettled by this one smile in a way I had never been before. There is an unwritten code between the journalist and his subjects in these situations. The journalist observes, the subject is observed. The journalist is active, the subject is passive. But this smile had turned the tables on that tacit agreement. Without uttering a single word, the man had posed a question that cut to the heart of the relationship between me and him, between us and them, between the rich world and the poor world. If he was embarrassed to be found weakened by hunger and ground down by conflict, how should I feel to be standing there so strong and confident?

I resolved there and then that I would write the story of Gufgaduud with all the power and purpose I could muster. It seemed at the time, and still does, the only adequate answer a reporter can give to the man's question.

I have one regret about that brief encounter in Gufgaduud. Having searched through my notes and studied the dispatch that the BBC broadcast, I see that I never found out what the man's name was. So, my nameless friend, if you are still alive, I owe you one.

¹ revulsion = disgust    ² inured = hardened

## Student 1

This student gets off on the wrong track by not focusing on the question. What are the key words of the question?

> George Alagiah is a television journalist reporting the war in Somalia which is in Africa. He won an award for his report because it was so shocking. The passage shows what is so shocking about the war. For example, he tells the story of Amina who searches for roots but when she comes back one of her daughters is dead.

This paragraph shows some understanding of the 'challenges' mentioned in the question, but it needs developing. Rewrite the paragraph to boost the grade.

> It must be terrible being a TV person because you want to help but you can't really you just have to take pictures and write. Alagiah shows this terrible situation by describing how pictures 'that stun editors' eventually become boring.

> He sometimes writes like he is telling a story, 'There was Amina... There was the old woman'. But it is a terrible story. And the suffering he faces is summed up in the 'face that I will never forget'. The man's smile is very confusing for the reporter, he doesn't know what kind of smile it was, but he is thinking hard about it so it must be important, and it 'touches me'. I think he is saying that the man was embarrassed and that challenged him.

How could the student develop the final point in this paragraph by showing the effect of the quotation?

> He made a connection with Alagiah, which was difficult for him, 'how should I feel to be standing there so strong and confident?'

This paragraph on language needs a lot of work to boost the student's grade. Rewrite it by:
– making a series of points about the language of the text
– developing them
– linking them

> Alagiah's language is very rich, e.g. 'revulsion', and 'inured'. He is describing the scene in a very detailed way, so he picks the right words, like 'festering wound the size of my hand'.

> So the piece shows lots of challenges faced by the writer.

How could you improve the final paragraph?

# The examiner's view

This answer shows some grasp of the text, but it is let down by not focusing on the key words of the question which are 'the challenges faced by television journalists reporting scenes of suffering'. The student makes some points and refers to the text but the points are of uneven quality and they need to be developed further with more detailed comments on the effect of the quotations. The conclusion is too brief to be truly effective.

## A low grade C

> **17** Assess your own answer against this C grade answer. Look at the 'Steps to success in reading' on page 7 to check how well you are meeting the assessment objectives. What do you need to work on to improve your grade?

## Student 2

This passage brings out the conflict between George Alagiah's emotional responses as a human being to what he saw in Somalia and the challenges he faced in carrying out his job as a television journalist, which required him to seek images to boost viewing figures.

He likens his hunt for the best picture to 'the craving for a drug'. He needs to get better (that is, more shocking) pictures to satisfy this craving, because a journalist is only as good as his last picture. He is aware how awful this is because he describes the hunt as 'ghoulish'. Furthermore he uses a string of adjectives to create a picture that does justice to what he has seen and show just how deprived and victimised these people are – 'hungry, lean, scared and betrayed'. His feelings are intensified by a sense of helplessness; his job is to report the suffering, not provide the help so desperately needed in 'a place the aid agencies had yet to reach.' What is more important, to give aid, or report the facts truthfully to the outside world?

This cannot be an easy job for anyone, as the physical and emotional drain must be overwhelming. He has to physically trawl 'from one hut to another'. He writes about his physical movements around Somalia to show the huge scale of the poverty and the vast numbers of people affected. The emotional demands are worse. 'A famine of quiet suffering and lonely death' is the way he described the slow death of two young children. Words such as 'quiet ... lonely' evoke pathos and allow his readers not only to empathise with him, but to picture the dying. This brings the emotion and pain to his writing which makes it so compelling. He describes the scene in a way that allows the readers to imagine it, but juxtaposes this with his own viewpoint. For example, 'this sounds callous, but it is just a fact of life' shows how detached he has become: 'the journalist observes, the subject is observed'.

The student has used the bullet points in the question well to structure the answer. Explain how.

This word means feelings of sadness and pity. Correctly used, technical terms could add to the quality of your answer. Can you find any other examples of technical terms used in this answer?

Notice how a point is:

1. made
2. supported by quotation
3. explained
4. developed further.

Where else does the student use this method later in the paragraph?

The student has used connecting words to link the ideas, so the whole answer flows. Find another example of this.

The whole passage leads up to the smile; the smile that disturbed a tough reporter 'accustomed to the evidence of deprivation'. ==He uses rhetorical questions to show his confusion about the smile and also he questions himself 'What was it about that smile?' He does not say 'a smile' but 'that smile', emphasising it; 'that' smile was the one that caused him to feel unnerved and confused – and eventually led him to write this piece – because it had turned the tables on the 'tacit agreement' between subject and the interviewer, on which journalism depends.== That one split second seemed to personify the difference and the divide between the haves and have nots. 'He was embarrassed to be found in his condition.' This quotation emphasises the gap between the observer and the observed; the passive and the active.

Overall, language is used to re-inforce the points he makes. He uses dramatic literary devices such as rhetorical questions, and also dashes, to question himself and present informal asides: 'How could it be? – but it was a smile nonetheless.' Short sharp sentences are used to grab our attention 'And then there was the face I will never forget.' ==However==, the last two paragraphs are my favourites. Here he first states why he has chosen to write about the 'nameless man' and his smile, which reminds us of his personal experience. Then he slips into a more informal tone: 'So, my nameless friend, if you are still alive, I owe you one.' This presents his thanks towards the smiling man for what he did and at the same time criticises himself for never asking his name.

In conclusion I feel that George Alagiah is a very clever man with a stylised way of presenting his experiences. He talks about a very taboo subject with such depth of emotion it engages the readers and makes them think and feel about his dilemma.

## The examiner's view

This is a very good answer because it shows excellent understanding and interpretation of the passage. It has addressed the question directly, and it has used the bullet points in the question well to give it structure. It analyses with great skill the ways in which the writer has used language, employing technical terms appropriately where necessary. There is a wide range of relevant points backed up with a good use of quotations.

**A grade A***

**18** Assess your own answer against this A* grade answer. Look at the 'Steps to success in reading' on page 7 to check how well you are meeting the assessment objectives. What do you need to work on to improve your grade?

# G Writing to argue, persuade, advise

By the end of this section you will have sharpened three skills that will help you to improve your answer to the writing question:

**1** show awareness of the audience and purpose of the task

**2** develop your points effectively

**3** give your writing impact.

You will also explore answers at different grades and assess your skills through writing an answer to a question similar to the one you will meet in the exam.

**IN THE EXAM:**
**SPECIFICATIONS A and B**

- There is one writing task. You can choose from two questions.
- The writing task will test your skills in writing to argue, persuade, advise.
- This question is worth 10% of your total mark for GCSE English.
- You must answer the question in 40 minutes.
- A third of the marks for this question are awarded for using a range of sentence structures effectively, and for accuracy of punctuation and spelling.
- Your answer to this task will be assessed against Writing assessment objectives (i), (ii) and (iii). See page 8.

## Writing to argue, persuade, advise

This type of writing always involves **influencing** your reader in some way. You might be:

❖ **arguing** a point of view (this could be the text for a speech)

❖ **persuading** someone to act in a certain way (this could be a letter to a friend)

❖ **advising** someone to follow a course of action (this could be from the advice section of a magazine, or an advice leaflet).

## What is the examiner looking for?

Below are the characteristics of a good answer and of a weak answer. Find the pairs of comments that match. This activity will focus your attention on the qualities that will gain you marks in this section of the exam. The first one has been done for you.

| A good answer | A weak answer |
|---|---|
| • is written in a tone that suits the audience and purpose | • is written in a tone that suits how you feel about the topic |

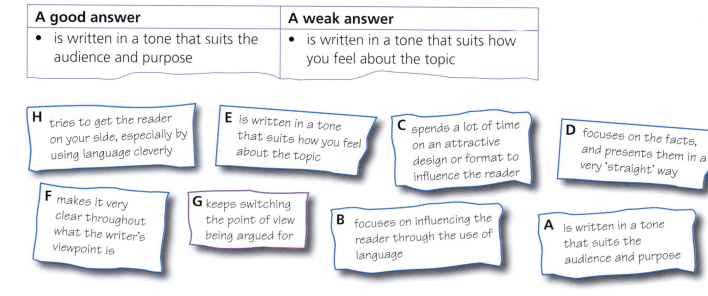

**H** tries to get the reader on your side, especially by using language cleverly

**E** is written in a tone that suits how you feel about the topic

**C** spends a lot of time on an attractive design or format to influence the reader

**D** focuses on the facts, and presents them in a very 'straight' way

**F** makes it very clear throughout what the writer's viewpoint is

**G** keeps switching the point of view being argued for

**B** focuses on influencing the reader through the use of language

**A** is written in a tone that suits the audience and purpose

Pieces of writing that argue, persuade and advise share many features, because they all aim to influence the reader. However, their different **purposes** mean that they demand a different approach by the writer.

1 Some of the features of writing to argue, persuade and advise are jumbled up in the boxes below. Draw up a table like the one started here, and complete it with the correct features in each column.

| | Argue | Persuade | Advise |
|---|---|---|---|
| *Purpose* | To present and develop a point of view about an issue | | |
| *Tone* | | Usually works on the reader's feelings to get the desired result | |
| *Technique* | | | Includes commands and words which suggest possibilities |

**Purpose**

To influence someone to do something, e.g. to buy an iPod

To present and develop a point of view about an issue, e.g. that the voting age should be reduced to 16

To give suggestions about a course of action, e.g. deciding on a career

**Tone**

A sympathetic and understanding tone

Usually logical and rational, which appeals to reasons and evidence

Usually works on the reader's feelings to get the desired result

**Some techniques**

Includes commands, and words which suggest possibilities, e.g. 'can', 'would', 'might', 'if … then'

Uses rhetorical techniques (tricks writers use to influence the reader), e.g. directly addressing audience, exaggeration, lists of three (see also page 136 below).

Presents points clearly, giving reasons and evidence and further detail

**EXAM TIP**

You can include *rhetorical techniques* in writing to *argue* as well as writing to *persuade*. (Also sometimes in advice writing, to get a point across very firmly.)

The difference between arguments and persuasive writing is mainly one of tone: think carefully about how reasonable (for 'argue') or pushy (for 'persuade') your writing should be.

2 Now read the extracts from student answers on pages 131. Identify the purpose, tone and techniques of each one by referring to your table. Which extracts are writing to argue, which to persuade and which to advise?

## Student 1

If you're worried about the kind of people who come to St Laurence's, you can relax. There is such a wide variety – different ages, sexes, faiths and backgrounds – that you are bound to find loads of kids that you can make friends with.

If you do choose this school, and you are lucky enough to get accepted, then here's three important things to keep in mind:

• Don't worry about the homework. They start you off slowly. You'll get used to it.

## Student 2

Ever wanted to help make a change in someone's life for the better? Well here's your opportunity to give back something to this community by volunteering at the local old people's home!

You might not be aware, but thousands of old people throughout the British Isles are just sitting, or lying in bed, at this very moment, being tortured by the insufferable loneliness that they have to put up with, day in and day out. By giving up just a couple of hours of your free time each week, you could make a huge difference to an elderly person's life. Company and companionship. That's not a lot to ask is it?

## Student 3

I recently had a cousin who died of cancer. He was eternally optimistic even when he had almost gone. I owe it to him that I should give money. Who do you owe it to? It could be your cousin or perhaps your mother. It might be your sibling, your grandparent or your friend. It might even be someone else who you did not realise impacted your life – a friendly smile, a kind look.

All of us owe it to them and to the unborn. We have already been cursed to live in a world with constant fear and danger of being ill. Let us save them from being born into this kind of world. Please give your money to this very worthwhile charity.

## Student 4

As teenagers, we all remember vividly the arguments that were brought up on every aspect of living. We were sometimes so furious that we took a vow of silence, saying we would never speak to them again. Of course, that was soon broken, as soon as we got hungry or needed more spending money. Those were the days when, no matter how big or how long the argument was, it was soon forgotten after a hug and an apology.

Yes, I do believe that these conflicts we have all had with our parents are the bond which brings father and son, mother and daughter, closer together. Where else can you develop the important life skills of arguing and fighting for your rights, in an atmosphere of such safety that when it all goes wrong you can go and cosy up in bed?

# Make your tone fit the audience

The tone of your writing will also depend on the audience. The audience will usually be named in the question – make sure you keep them in mind throughout your writing. For example:

❖ advice to the school governors will have to be formal and serious in tone

❖ advice to fellow teenagers will be less formal and can be humorous.

---

**3** Read the exam question below, then study the student's response.

**(a)** Explain why the tone does not suit the audience. Point to at least two examples in the text of phrases that should not be used.

**(b)** Rewrite the letter in a more appropriate tone to improve its grade.

---

Write a letter to your local newspaper to put forward your views about a controversial planning decision.

---

I am writing to you to share my views about the new supermarket. To start off with I am going to tell you my reasons against the supermarket. Reason 1 is my mum doesn't shop at Supasave because they don't sell kid's clothes. I think it's a disgrace that Kidz is going. Reason 2 could be that Supasave Supermarket is humungous! We're just a tiddly place and we've got enough problems with parking anyway.

I say cut the council tax and make the car parks free first. Chuck this idea out.

Cheers

Disgusted of Swanbridge

# 2 Develop your points effectively

When you write to argue, persuade or advise, you need to give more than just a series of short statements or opinions. These are too brief to influence the audience. Instead, you must *develop* your points to make them convincing.

## Collecting ideas

You have to collect your points, of course, before you can develop them. This is why *planning* your answer is so essential. When you plan, you are jotting down your main ideas, then putting them into a sensible order. You should spend no more than a few minutes doing this.

> **4** Read the exam question below, then study the plans that two students made.
>    **(a)** What are the good points of plan A that helped the student write an A grade answer?
>    **(b)** What should the student writing plan B do to improve from a grade C? For example, would it be easy to get a paragraph plan from these notes?

> Argue **either** for **or** against the idea that some jobs and careers are only suitable for girls and some for boys.

**Plan A**

> intro – all careers suitable for both sexes
> 1   Girls can be just as strong – eg Kelly Holmes, Ellen MacArthur
> 2   Boys can be just as sensitive – eg writers, singers
> 3   Equal opportunities laws are important – contrast with the past
> conc – my sister is engineer, and me...?

**Plan B**

| agree | disagree |
|---|---|
| Girls can't do some jobs<br>Girls are naturally more emotional and caring | Boys and girls should have equal opportunities<br>Good training and equipment can open up jobs to both genders |

> **5** Look at the exam question again. Add two or three more points to student A's plan.

## Developing your points

It is a good idea to begin each paragraph with a key point or opinion. You can then develop this point in the remaining sentences in the paragraph. Developing a point can mean:

✓ giving one or more reasons for your opinion
✓ going into your point in more detail
✓ giving one or more examples
✓ providing some evidence, e.g. facts and figures, personal experience, quotations.

**6** Study how this A grade student has developed some of the points into paragraphs. What key points are being made in each paragraph? How are they developed?

> Girls are perfectly able nowadays to cope with the demands of a 'male' world. They are often stereotyped as being weaker physically and less able to make decisions, but sportswomen, like Kelly Holmes and Ellen MacArthur, who sailed single handed around the world, have proved that this is no longer true. With the right equipment and training there is little that a woman can't do and a man can.
>
> Boys are also quite capable of doing so-called women's jobs. The kitchen is the traditional place for a woman, yet the cook who has made the most impact on the way school children eat is Jamie Oliver. The problem is partly labelling the jobs as 'men's' or 'women's' in the first place – this sets up a false distinction.

**7** 'You have been asked to advise the school governors on changes that are needed to your school or college to make it more attractive and provide a better learning environment.'

The student below has presented a series of points, but hasn't developed them. Help the student push the answer to a C grade or better by developing three of the points made.

Refer to the checklist on the previous page for help if necessary.

> I am here today to tell you that I believe there should be many changes to help students.
>
> First I believe we should redecorate the school.
>
> It would be a good idea to introduce some new subjects in the curriculum that are more relevant to the students. And teaching methods need to be looked at, so that students can have more modern ways of learning things.
>
> You could also look into methods of making people want to come to school.
>
> The school rules need to be looked at as many are out of date.

## Using paragraphs

The most important way of giving your writing structure is to use paragraphs to organise your key points.

*Linking* your paragraphs will boost your grade even more. This means referring back to the paragraph before when you begin a new one. It makes your writing, and your argument, flow. Two good ways of linking your paragraphs are to:

☑ use 'signposting' words or 'connectives' such as 'Another point is', 'However', 'Of course…'

☑ repeat (or echo) the words or sentence structure of the previous paragraph.

**8** Look back at the student's answer in activity 6 (page 134). How has the student linked the two paragraphs effectively?

**9** Look back at the three points you developed in activity 7 (page 134). Have you given each a separate paragraph? Have you linked them effectively by using one of the methods from the checklist at the bottom of page 134.

If necessary, redraft them to make the structure of your writing even more impressive and effective.

## Beginnings and endings

**10** On the left below are some opening sentences for the task in activity 7 on page 134. Match the openings with the descriptions on the right below. Which opening do you think would be most effective?

| Opening sentences | Types of opening |
|---|---|
| 1. I wonder whether you have strolled round the school recently? | A) Use of contrast for rhetorical effect |
| 2. There is a direct link between the quality of the school environment and the quality of the work produced within it. | B) Anecdote (personal experience) |
| 3. Last term I was asked to show a visitor from abroad round the college, and I was ashamed. | C) Direct challenge in the form of a question |
| 4. I'm sure we all take great pride in keeping our homes well-decorated; why can we not show the same respect for our school? | D) Straight statement of view |

**11** Match the concluding sentences on the left below with the descriptions of different endings on the right. Which conclusion do you think would be most effective? Give your reasons.

| Concluding sentences | Types of conclusion |
|---|---|
| 1. Therefore my advice would be to implement the measures described above, or risk harming the school's reputation. | A) A summary of the main points of the essay |
| 2. You as governors have to ask yourselves: can we afford not to make urgent improvements to the school's environment? | B) A stark choice presented through contrasting alternatives |
| 3. I therefore recommend three things: re-decoration of the main block; replacement of old art equipment; new display boards throughout. | C) A challenge to the audience in form of a question |

## 3 Give your writing impact

Writing to argue, persuade and advise must have impact because its main purpose is to influence the reader.

## Using rhetorical devices

Rhetorical devices are techniques to persuade the reader to agree with the writer's point of view. When you are writing to argue or persuade, rhetorical devices can add a lot of impact.

> **12** Read the rhetorical devices described in boxes 1–5 below. Match them up to extracts A–H taken from student essays on pages 139–141.

**A**
It isn't just the physical damage, though, there is damage to the mind as well, and sometimes to society itself.

**1 Rhetorical questions** – questions that are asked for effect, not really to get an answer, e.g. 'Are we really going to stand by and let this happen?

**2 Varied sentence lengths** – a short sentence after a long one can give added impact to a point. Like this.

**E**
The world of games is a simulation of the real world, a fake, a substitute.

**B**
Every day parents are buying games to keep their children occupied. Fine. But do they check the rating? Not always.

**3 Sound effects** – including *alliteration* (using the same sound at the start of words), e.g. 'a neighbourhood nuisance', and *repetition* of the same word or phrase, e.g. 'Today … today … today'.

**F**
Have you heard of an 18 year old going on a 'Grand Theft Auto' rampage stealing cars, killing people for fun?

**4 Direct address** – using pronouns such as 'you' and 'we' to engage the audience directly.

**C**
Now you, sensible teenagers, are too mature to be influenced, but children are impressionable.

**5 Groups of three** – often listing three examples makes your point forceful and stylish.

**G**
That is improving your life, it is keeping you healthy, you meet new people and you have FUN.

**D**
And why not play a board game with your younger sibling? Or even try to talk to your mum?

**H**
This can help children because it keeps them out of trouble, it keeps them entertained and they also learn new things.

# Make your points clear

Although rhetorical devices are very effective and will help you gain marks, you must also focus on making your points as clear as possible. Two ways of doing this are:

❖ **linking your sentences** effectively with 'signpost' phrases and words (e.g. 'however', 'on the other hand', 'surely', 'furthermore')

❖ paying attention to **punctuation**. Each sentence must make sense, and must end with a full stop, question or exclamation mark.

> Remember that when you are making a new point, it is usually better to start a new sentence. Don't just add commas and write down your thoughts as they occur to you:
>
> *If we made the place look more pleasant then the students would be happier, in particular the corridors need decorating.* ✗
>
> *If we made the place look more pleasant, then the students would be happier. In particular, the* <mark>corridors</mark> *need decorating.* ✓

Add comma to show end of this clause

Add comma to show pause after the opening phrase

New subject, so begin a new sentence

**13** Read the two student answers below. The content is the same, but student 1 has written a grade A response because the ideas are expressed clearly.

Explain what is missing from student 2's response, and why that makes it a low grade C. Refer to the students' use of:
  ■ signposting
  ■ punctuation.

## Student 1

Dear Editor

As was indicated in the report in last Friday's edition of your paper, the council has given into the corporate might of SupaSave Supermarkets to allow a development in the centre of our town.

This will not only ruin local shops and businesses, like the chemists and 'Kidz', the only children's clothes shop in the area, but it will also entail destroying shop fronts that date back hundreds of years. In addition the development is so big it will be completely out of keeping with the rest of our small town. In any case, if you need to shop at a supermarket, most of the major ones have stores within a few miles of Swanbridge.

**Student 2**

*Dear Editor*

*As was indicated in the report in last Friday's edition of your paper the council has given into the might of SupaSave Supermarkets to allow a development in the centre of our town, this will ruin local shops and businesses like the chemists and 'Kidz' the only children's clothes shop in the area. It will also entail destroying shop fronts that date back hundreds of years, the development is so big it will be completely out of keeping with the rest of our small town, if you need to shop, at a supermarket most of the major ones have stores within a few miles of Swanbridge.*

**14** Read the extract below, which was written as part of a leaflet aimed at raising money for the RSPCA. Help this student boost the answer's grade from D to a C or better by giving the writing impact. Rewrite the response to:
  ■ include rhetorical devices
  ■ make it clearer, paying attention to signposting and punctuation.

*The need for the RSPCA's services is steadily increasing, in 2000 RSPCA Inspectors looked at 126,746 complaints of cruelty to animals. And it's not just because of bad treatment of animals in the home many animals suffer through pollution and poisoning etc. and when they are brought to us in a bad way we need to be able to look after them in refuges – we need money to keep the animal hospitals and clinics (52 of them) going.*

# 4 Work with student answers

You are now going to pull together all the learning you have done in this section by attempting a complete writing task. You will then study two other students' answers for comparison.

**15 (a)** First answer the exam question below. You have 40 minutes.

    **(b)** Then read the students' answers and examiner's comments below. Complete the activities in the boxes.

> Your class is going to debate whether computer games are a dangerous waste of time or have the potential to change people's lives for the better.
>
> Write the text for a speech you would make in this debate, arguing either in favour of or against the playing of computer games.

## Student 1

1   Hello. I'm going to argue in favour of computer games.

    When people complaen about computer games what they really mean is that vilence in games is somehow making children behave vilently but have you heard of an 18 year old going on a 'Grand Theft Auto' rampage
5   stealing cars, killing people for fun?

    Games can change peoples lives for the better because it can:
    1) get people into new sports e.g. tennis
    2) it can stop children being unrully as they have something to do
    3) they can be educational and help children to learn

10   Computer games can get **you** into new activities as **you** might be given a game like 'Fifa world cup 2006' or 'NHL 2K6'. **You** may not even realise the sport exists but **you** may get into the game so much **you** want to join a club. That is improving **your** life, it is keeping **you** healthy, **you** meet new people and **you** have FUN.

15   Computer games keeps children amused and with a little child if you buy them a new game it will keep them occupied so they wont cause trouble and with bigger children they can see what happens from vilence and it can put them off it but also it keeps them occupied and off the streets. This can help children because it keeps them out of trouble and it keeps them
20   entertained and they also learn new things.

    Computer games can educate people as if they are trying to learn a new language they can remember what each topic is and change the language and learn new words. **Also** children use computer games to help them rember things like they could use a football game to rember countries
25   or to help them rember a foreign language. **Also** educational games are

---

Why is this a weak opening?

Most of this student's points are developed quite well, but the point in this paragraph is not. Can you develop it?

This student has thought about the structure of the answer. How can you tell?
However, numbered lists are rarely a good idea. Here it stops the flow of the speech. Can you make this section more effective?

Good use of the second person pronoun 'you'. Where else does the student use this device?

Each paragraph adds a useful new point to the argument, but the writing needs to be punchier for a speech. Add two rhetorical devices to this paragraph.

'Also' is a signpost word saying 'here's another point', but it's overused in this essay. Replace the two examples here with different signposts.

produced for little children helping them to read, count etc. These can help little children get a head start in basic subjects and it can help adults learn new languages or countries.

**30** Real life isn't a better idea than playing computer games as you can make mistakes that cost loads. You could spend hundreds of pounds on kit for a sport only to find out you don't like it whereas you need only could spend fourty pound for a computer game to find out if you like it. Also it makes more jobs as there has to be people to make the computer games and quite a lot of people would love to create a video game and get paid for it.

**35** Also with computer games you have to use your brain which can improve how you solve problems and how you cope with pressure as in some computer games you get pressure to complete the level and not let the team down and you approach things in different ways e.g. 'All guns blazing' or 'Slow and Steady' and you learn what approach fits what problem best.

**40** I think computer games help peoples lives as they are educational, fun and it gives people something to do. Most people who say they are bad don't know what they are talking about and don't like computer games for one reason or another.

> Make this point clearer by breaking the paragraph up into sentences and punctuating them effectively.

> The last paragraph does sum up the speech, but it has no impact. How could you help the student to sway the audience?

## The examiner's view

The achievement here is mixed. The argument is quite well developed with good ideas, but spelling, punctuation and grammar are erratic. Some parts work well as a speech, others do not. It is carefully but rather unimaginitively structured. To improve the grade the candidate needs to be more aware of the purpose and audience of the writing, use more interesting sentence structures and vocabulary, and pay more attention to spelling, punctuation and grammar.

### A grade C

> **16** Assess your own answer against this C grade answer. Look at the 'Steps to success in writing' on page 9 to check how well you are meeting the assessment objectives. What do you need to work on to improve your grade?

### Student 2

> This is a strong opening which immediately shows an awareness of the audience. Explain how.

**1** Fellow students, how many of you enjoy playing computer games? Quite a lot I imagine! Many young people – and for that matter, some adults too – own a Playstation, X Box, Gameboy ... and so on. But just how much time do you – and they - spend twiddling a joystick or tapping away on a **5** controller? How many of you will develop eye strain, a bad back, repetitive strain injury? It isn't just the physical damage, though, there is damage to the mind as well, and, sometimes to society itself.

> The student uses a humorous tone at times. Find another example in the essay. Explain how the humour helps to make a serious point.

It isn't all bad, of course. Some computer games are harmless, enjoyable, even educational. But not even the most ardent fan could claim that **10** 'Vampire Revenge Bloodbath' (or whatever the latest violence obsessed game is called) is healthy. We have all seen the newspaper stories about the loner, who stabbed an innocent bystander because they 'saw it in a film'. The same thing applies to games. The virtual world could fuse with the real one and the dazed and pixel-drugged addict could cause another

15  needless death. The victim is a matter of chance – a stranger, a friend, a member of your own family...

And if a supposedly rational grown up can be corrupted by violent scenes played on a small screen, what about children? Every day parents are buying games to keep their children occupied. Fine. But do they check the

20  rating? Not always. Primary children, no older than eight or even less, can be killing virtual enemies for hours on end, making them more inclined to be violent to anyone who crosses their path. Now you, sensible teenagers, are too mature to be influenced, but children are impressionable. A child is not ready for an 18 rated war game; to them, games like these can

25  be taken as truth. Who wants their son or perhaps even their daughter believing it is fun to kill? Remember the James Bulger case.

It is also worth considering the less extreme effects of computer games. Someone who is sitting on a sofa with a controller in their hands is not exercising anything other than their fingers. They are not getting fresh air,

30  they are not interacting with anybody and they are probably not learning anything other than how to keep their character alive for one more level. Playing computer games can contribute to health problems. Obesity, for a start, is an increasing problem for teenagers as well as the rest of society. As they grow older they will become easy prey to anything from heart

35  disease to diabetes. The social consequences can also be dire; a race of people may be created who can't relate to the real world.

Let's get this into perspective. Half an hour playing a computer game is not going to ruin your life, but surely kicking a football around instead is much healthier. And why not play a board game with your younger sibling?

40  Or even try to talk to your mum? The world of games is a simulation of the real world, a fake, a substitute. Now wouldn't you prefer the genuine article?

The student use a wide and varied vocabulary to good effect. Can you find other examples?

Look at the way the writer varies the length of these sentences. What effect does it have? Where else is this technique used in the essay?

Notice how each paragraph discusses a different point. Draw up what may have been this student's plan for the essay.

A strong finish, with three rhetorical questions. What are their effect here? Where else does the student use this technique?

## The examiner's view

You may not agree with the views expressed, but this is very strongly argued. Look at how well it is organised into paragraphs and at the powerful opening and conclusion. You can also tell it would work well as a speech to a class. It is very ambitious in expression, especially in the way it varies sentences, shows real individuality in the language, and uses a range of punctuation. Spelling is consistently accurate across a wide vocabulary.

**A grade A***

17  Assess your own answer against this A* grade answer. Look at the 'Steps to success in writing' on page 9 to check how well you are meeting the assessment objectives. What do you need to work on to improve your grade?

## 5 Exam question practice

Now is the time to put everything in this section into practice for yourself.

**Remember** that you cannot practise too much. Areas such as planning, beginning and ending powerfully and giving your writing impact will improve very quickly when you practise.

**18** Allow 40 minutes, and choose one of the questions below. When you have finished, assess yourself against your answer to the question in Activity 15, or swap your work with your partner's and assess each other's. Look back at the 'Steps to success in writing' on page 9 to identify exactly where you are doing well and where you need to improve. Note down three areas in which you would like to improve, and practise those skills.

## EXAM TIP

- Think carefully about the audience and purpose of the task. Are you writing to argue, persuade or advise?
- Draw up a plan of your key points or opinions. Then make sure you develop these points in your answer.
- Make your points clear by signposting and punctuating your sentences.
- Give your writing impact by including powerful words and rhetorical devices (if appropriate).
- Make sure you check your spelling, punctuation and use of sentences.

**1** 'Computer games have the potential to change people's lives for the better.'

'Getting involved in real life is better than playing brain-dead computer games.'

Argue the case either in favour of or against the playing of computer games.

*(Higher Tier)*

**2** A local newspaper has asked readers for ideas on how to improve the environment in your area.

Write a letter to the newspaper, giving your ideas and advice on this subject.

*(Higher Tier)*

**3** 'Girls lack physical strength; boys are not caring. We should be honest; some jobs and careers are only suitable for girls, and some for boys.'

Argue either for or against the view that some jobs and careers are only suitable for girls, and some for boys.

*(Foundation Tier)*

**4** The government is very concerned about truancy and underachieving students.

Write a persuasive letter to the Minister of Education outlining your ideas for making school or college more attractive to students.

Your letter should include points on the following topics:

❖ improvements to buildings, decoration, food service, facilities

❖ the curriculum, including the range of subjects available

❖ teaching methods

❖ ideas for motivating students

❖ school or college rules.

*(Foundation Tier)*

# H Writing to analyse, review, comment

By the end of this section you will have sharpened three skills that will help you to improve your answer to this writing question:

1 take account of audience and purpose in your writing

2 present a well-structured and balanced answer

3 use language in a convincing and effective way.

You will also explore answers at different grades and assess your skills through writing an answer to a question similar to the one you will meet in the exam.

## IN THE EXAM:
### SPECIFICATIONS A and B

- There is one writing task. You can choose from two questions.

- The writing task will test your skills in writing to analyse, review, comment.

- This question is worth 10% of your total mark for GCSE English.

- You must answer the question in 40 minutes.

- A third of the marks for this question are awarded for using a range of sentence structures effectively, and for accuracy of the punctuation and spelling.

- Your answer to this task will be assessed against Writing assessment objectives (i), (ii) and (iii). See page 8.

## Writing to analyse, review, comment

When you write to analyse, review or comment:

❖ the purpose is often to help someone understand an issue or situation

❖ you usually take a balanced view, e.g. covering different choices or discussing views for and against an issue

❖ the tone is often formal and unemotional.

## What is the examiner looking for?

Below are the characteristics of a good answer and of a weak answer. Find the pairs of comments that match. This activity will focus your attention on the qualities that will gain you marks in this section of the exam. The first one has been done for you.

| A good answer | A weak answer |
|---|---|
| • focuses on the key words of the question, especially the audience and purpose | • uses the question just as a starting point for writing about whatever comes most naturally |

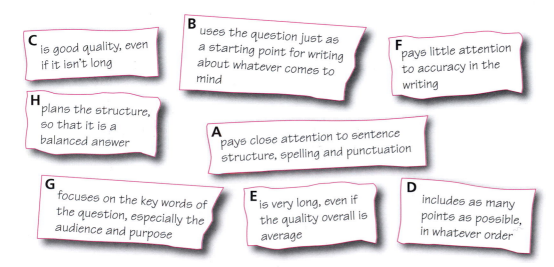

**C** is good quality, even if it isn't long

**B** uses the question just as a starting point for writing about whatever comes to mind

**F** pays little attention to accuracy in the writing

**H** plans the structure, so that it is a balanced answer

**A** pays close attention to sentence structure, spelling and punctuation

**G** focuses on the key words of the question, especially the audience and purpose

**E** is very long, even if the quality overall is average

**D** includes as many points as possible, in whatever order

## 1 Take account of audience and purpose in your writing

### Identifying purpose and audience

Each of the three types of writing – analyse, review, comment – has a slightly different purpose. To achieve a good grade, you need to have a clear idea about the purpose of the task.

When you **analyse** something you look at it closely, you examine it. Analysis is concerned with looking closely at details and examining the evidence.

When you analyse you often need to discuss a wide range of facts and opinions, and give a balanced view about an issue.

When you **review** something you discuss it. You probably pass a judgement on it or evaluate it, and you give your readers a careful opinion.

You might write a review of a book or a film, or you might review your decision to choose to study German instead of geography.

When you **comment** on something you give your opinion on something, or you comment on other people's opinions. Like a football commentator, you will tell your audience what is happening, but also comment on events.

You usually express your opinion in a cool, unemotional way.

Look for the key word in the question that tells you the **purpose** of the writing. Often it will be 'analyse', 'review' or 'comment'. Then look for any other key words. They will tell you what the **topic** of the writing is, or who the **audience** is.

> **1** Read the three examination questions below. Identify the key words in each question. Which one gives you the purpose of the writing? The first one has been done for you.

These are the topics you have to write about.

These words show your purpose – to give a balanced view. You are being asked to analyse the topic.

**A** 'Some people are best living in a large, noisy, active family environment; other people do well living alone.'

What do you think are the advantages and disadvantages of each of these ways of life?

**B** 'A dog is a man's best friend.'

'Pets are a big responsibility, and can ruin your home and garden if you're not careful.'

Comment on these two views.

**C** 'School uniform is a great help to parents, and stops expensive competition amongst children, as well as giving the school an identity.'

'School uniform makes you look like a robot.'

Review the evidence for these, or any other, views on the issue of school uniforms, based on your own experience and on the views of others you have spoken to on the subject.

**EXAM TIP**

Note that the words 'analyse', 'review' or 'comment' do not always have to occur in the question, but the wording of the question will make it clear what kind of writing you have to do.

# Make your writing suit audience and purpose

How do you write with the audience and purpose in mind? If you can take account of the following factors in your writing, you will be well on the way to boosting your grade.

**Thinking about audience and purpose will have an effect on...**

☑ The **tone** of your writing.
Formal or informal? Serious or humorous? Chatty or detached? You use a less formal tone when you write to a friend than when you write to a newspaper.

☑ The **viewpoint** of your writing.
Sometimes you are asked to write as a teenager, or as someone interested in a particular topic, e.g. sport. Imagine you are this person as you write.

☑ The **form** of your writing.
You may be asked to write a letter – so structure it as a letter. You may be asked to write the text of a speech – so address the audience listening to you.

☑ The **content** of your writing.
Make sure this is relevant to the purpose of the task. Look at the topic given in the question.

**2** Look at the exam question below. The student has started to make a checklist of the points to think about, and some short notes. Complete these notes.

> A friend is thinking of leaving home. Write a letter to him or her reviewing the points that should be considered.

**Purpose:** *to review*

**Audience:** *friend*

**Tone:** *informal*

**Viewpoint:**

**Form:**

**Content:**

Because the audience is identified in the question ('a friend'), this helps you to decide on an appropriate tone – informal. You will write a letter which is grammatically correct, but its tone will be casual and relaxed.

*Remember* 'TV FC' and write this on your planning page. This will remind you to think about:

- Tone
- Viewpoint
- Form and
- Content.

If you think TV FC as you plan, your writing will suit the audience and purpose of the task.

## A TO A*

One way of raising your grade to A* is to adopt a really convincing tone in your answer and keep it going consistently. The most successful answers show a real sense of the audience, e.g. a letter to a friend will be informal.

## EXAM TIP

In the exam, you need not normally include your address or date at the top of the letter. The examiner is interested in whether you can write in appropriate tone and style, rather than in the details of setting the letter out.

**3** Look carefully at this exam question, then read the opening paragraphs of two student answers below. Which answer takes the audience and purpose into account and therefore achieves a higher grade? Use the checklist of points to consider on page 145 to help you.

Choose a book or film which you have recently enjoyed. Write the text for a talk, to be given to your class, reviewing the book or film.

In your speech you should consider:

❖ the subject matter of the film or book

❖ what you considered its strong aspects, and why it appealed to you

❖ any negative points

❖ why you might recommend the book or film to your class.

**Student 1**

When people go to the cinema to see the Da Vinci Code, they are probably full of excitement and anticipation, especially if they have read the book. It's one of those books that is very strong on plot and excitement, but not so strong on style – actually its style is atrocious. There are plenty of books like this – they call them page-turners, or airport books because you get them at the airport. So the audience is bound to imagine that the Da Vinci Code would make a fabulous film, but they would be in error. On the contrary, the director actually manages to make the story dull.

**Student 2**

When I went to the cinema to see the Da Vinci Code, I was full of excitement and anticipation, because I had just finished the book. It's one of those books that is very strong on plot and excitement, but not so strong on style, so I thought this would make a fabulous film, as that's what films are so good at – thrills and excitement. Never was I more wrong. Would you believe it, the director actually managed to make the story dull!

**4** Now it's time for you to practise writing with the audience and purpose in mind. Write the first paragraph of your answer to the following question. Remember to identify audience and purpose by picking out the key words in the question.

You will need to consider the following:

Think of a suitable headline

■ how can I show immediately that I am writing an article for a magazine?

Start with different attitudes towards exam revision among teenagers. Use colloquial, informal tone and language.

■ how can I engage my readers – teenagers – through the topics I choose and the language I use?

'Some people are driven by ambition; others take life as it comes.'

Write an article for a teenage magazine commenting on what you think are the advantages and disadvantages of each of these attitudes.

**5** Swap your paragraph with a partner's. Check that their tone, viewpoint, form and content (TV FC) suit the audience and purpose of the task. Make two or three constructive comments on your partner's answer.

Listen to your partner's comments and rewrite your own paragraph if necessary.

## 2 Present a well-structured and balanced answer

Examiners want to see that you organise your ideas well. This means planning your writing and using paragraphs to give it structure.

When you analyse, review or comment, you are usually giving a careful and balanced view of a topic. It is particularly important to plan and structure your writing to achieve the balance.

## Planning your writing

A simple plan gives your work shape and purpose – and ensures that you stick to the point.

Planning can be broken down into two stages:

> 1 **Note down your first thoughts on the topic, in no particular order.**

> 2 **Shape, or edit, these ideas into a logical order.** You could organise the ideas into groups. Or you could put numbers against them to show the order of the paragraphs.

Now let's see how these two stages work in practice.

> **6** Read the exam question below, and look at the plans which three students have started.
>
> **(a)** Discuss with a partner the three different approaches to planning the answer to this question. What are the good points and bad points of each?
>
> **(b)** Having considered all three plans, which do you think is best for this question?

> Comment on the advantages and disadvantages of keeping pets.

**Student 1**

> *Pets – advantages & disadvantages*
>
> - *companionship, esp. for old people*
> - *exercise good for you*
> - *cost of vets' bills*
> - *too many animals in the world*
> - *children can learn to look after/take responsibility*
> - *they are left at home alone for long periods*
> - *add intro. and conclusion*

This student has jotted down thoughts as they occur

**EXAM TIP**

Planning your answer is very important, but don't spend too long on it – a few minutes should be enough.

**Student 2**

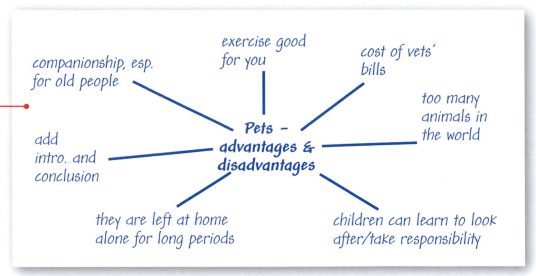

This student has drawn a spider diagram. The topic is at the centre, and the ideas are the 'legs'.

exercise good for you

companionship, esp. for old people

cost of vets' bills

too many animals in the world

Pets – advantages & disadvantages

add intro. and conclusion

they are left at home alone for long periods

children can learn to look after/take responsibility

**Student 3**

This student has recorded ideas in 2 columns

Pets

| advantages | disadvantages |
|---|---|
| companionship, esp. for old people | they are left at home alone for long periods |
| exercise good for you | too many animals in the world |
| children can learn to look after/ take responsibility | cost of vets' bills |

***Remember*** to use whichever method of planning suits you.
If you are given a 'for and against' type of question, you could use a simple 4-paragraph scheme:

- Paragraph 1: introduction
- Paragraph 2: Points in favour of x
- Paragraph 3: Points against x
- Paragraph 4: Conclusion.

**7** Read the exam question below, and the student's notes on each paragraph. Match each note to a paragraph number to create an effective plan for the student's answer.

'Being really alone for the first time.'

Write about this, analysing your thoughts and feelings at the time and since.

| | |
|---|---|
| Paragraph 1 | Analyse in detail my thoughts at the time. |
| Paragraph 2 | Looking at 'being alone' now, and concluding. |
| Paragraph 3 | How my feelings about this changed, with a new perspective as I got older. |
| Paragraph 4 | Introduction – set the scene of 'for the first time' experience. |

**8** The examiner will know immediately whether you have spent time planning your answer. Read these two student extracts, which begin answering the essay question on 'being really alone'. Match them to the correct examiner's comments.

## Student 1

*It was a weird experience, and one which I will never forget. My mum said afterwards, that she had meant to leave me, and did not realise that I would be frightened. At other times later in my life I quite liked being alone, though. Being alone is not always a bad experience, and can be quite good. When I first went on holiday on my own I really enjoyed it, but some of my friends were homesick...*

## Student 2

*I was first truly on my own when my Mum left me while she went out to the shops for a minute, and left her keys at home. She, of course, couldn't get back in, and I was too young to understand and to find them. I simply had the frightening sensation of being abandoned, on my own for the first time in my young life. This was terrifying, of course, but as I look back on this incident now I see things differently...*

### Examiner's comment a)

This extract doesn't suggest that any sort of planning has taken place. The first sentence doesn't make it clear what incident the student is going to be analysing. When is the 'first time'? The references to different periods in the writer's life are thrown together in a confusing way.

### Examiner's comment b)

This extract suggests that the student has thought hard about how to organise the essay. The first paragraph sets the scene, making it quite clear what incident the essay is going to analyse, but without going into too much detail. The final sentence signals how the student is going to organise the essay.

*Remember* to follow this two-stage planning process:

■ note down your thoughts
■ shape or edit them into a logical order.

**9** Plan your answer to the following exam question.

### Family holidays

Write a review of past holidays which you have taken with your family, highlighting the bad and the good memories.

# Writing strong openings and endings

The opening lines of your answer should:

☑ Get the reader's attention by making an early impact. Choose your words carefully, and think whether your sentences work together.

☑ Set the right tone. Get the appropriate level of formality. Think about the audience and purpose of the writing.

☑ Introduce both sides of an issue. Often the question has two sides. Show in your opening that you are considering both sides.

**10** Read this exam question. Then study the three different openings below. Put them in order of merit. Refer to the checklist above.

'Every individual has the freedom to choose whether or not to smoke.'

'Smoking is a menace to public health, and should be made illegal.'

Write a speech, for an audience of adults, commenting on these two views.

**Student 1**

My nan smokes, and it stinks the house out. She didn't always smoke, my mum says, but she's smoked as long as I've known her, smoking is disgusting. Smokers are drug-users, and should be treated as such, my nan says she isn't a drug-user, but I reckon she is. (Though she's not as bad as heroin users of course.)

**Student 2**

This is a matter of great national importance. The rights of the individual should be balanced against the good of society as a whole. When considered from this angle, it is very clear which conclusion we should come to. Simply in numerical terms, more people are affected adversely by someone smoking than the single person who gets a (supposed) benefit.

**Student 3**

If I took out a cigarette here and now, lit it, and smoked it in front of you, what am I doing? Am I exercising my right of personal freedom – the freedom to choose? Or am I endangering public health? These are the two principles that lie behind people's opposing views on the issue. My purpose tonight is to guide you through these views.

Endings are also very important. You should aim to round off your ideas, and bring your essay to a neat conclusion. Again, paying attention to your language and sentence structure will leave your reader with a good impression.

**11** Refer back to the exam question on smoking. Student 3 wrote a weak ending – shown below. Rewrite it to improve the mark.

**Hint:** Look back at the opening paragraph when you write your ending. Can you link them in some way?

So we come to the end of a very long and interesting discussion. I hope I have been able to keep your interest enough for you to understand that people are divided on the issue, and there are lots of different views.

# 3 Use language in a convincing and effective way

In this unit you will practise three skills to make your writing more convincing and effective – 'signposting' your writing, using rhetorical techniques and varying your sentences.

## Signposting your answer

'Signposting' means using words and phrases to show what point of view you are discussing, and how it fits into your answer overall. This has two benefits:

❖ it guides the reader (and the examiner) clearly through your answer

❖ it shows that you are taking a balanced and objective approach.

> **12** Read the last two paragraphs of this student essay (for the full essay, see page 155 below). The annotations highlight two signposts. Identify two other signposting words or phrases and say how they guide the reader, or highlight the student's point of view.

page 155 below

### Remember

- To signpost **additional or similar** points, use: 'as well', 'too', 'in addition', 'for example', 'another advantage is', 'what is more', 'furthermore', 'a further point in favour'.

- To signpost **opposing** points, use: 'yet', 'however', 'whereas', 'alternatively', 'on the other hand', 'by contrast', 'others might say', 'nevertheless'.

- To signpost your **ending**, use: 'in conclusion', 'to sum up', 'then', 'therefore'.

We always seem to link 'myth' with 'reality', and for me 'reality' is the essence of what cities offer. Cities are vibrant places, full of people working, relaxing, being tourists, rushing about, even just sitting and watching each other. For me, this is the point of a city, and it is at the heart of why I would make a city holiday my choice. On the other hand it could be said that cities are crowded, noisy, restless places which harbour criminals – but in a way that's their whole point (well, not the criminals, obviously). Therefore I feel drawn to the 'life' which every big city seems to generate, as though I am revitalised just by being part of the great whirl of humanity. Of course the famous cities have their famous attractions – there's only one Eiffel Tower or Empire State Building – but these only serve as a focal point for all the human activity which takes place around them.

I hope, then, that I have given my comments to you (and, I hope, to your reader) in a way which leaves no doubt about my choice. I would recommend the seaside to sun-worshippers; and perhaps the countryside to claustrophobics; but for me a City Centre is the centre of the world.

*Signposts on opposing view*

*Signposts a conclusion, or summing up*

# Including tricks and techniques

In examinations, don't play safe with language. Examiners like to see you trying out more ambitious words and expressions, even if you don't always get them right.

When reviewing or commenting, you can often liven up your style by using some of these techniques:

- ☑ **rhetorical questions**, where you ask a question to achieve an effect, not expecting an answer, e.g. 'Would you really expect anything different?'

- ☑ **'inclusive' phrases**, helpful if you want to involve your audience, e.g. 'You will have noticed that', or 'I'm sure we can all agree on one thing...'

- ☑ **listing points**, often in threes, e.g. 'Blood, sweat and tears'

- ☑ **exaggeration**, deliberately overstating something, to make your point clear, e.g. 'You will hear this view a thousand times a day'

- ☑ **contrast**, setting opposites against each other for effect, e.g. 'Cars give us great freedom, but they also bring huge costs to the planet'

- ☑ **varying language**, through the use of a rich vocabulary and very well chosen and apt phrases or words.

> **13** Match up the following extracts from a student essay with the tricks and techniques listed above. Then write a short comment explaining why this student's use of language gained a grade A.

**A** How can I reject the waves crashing on the beach, or the tranquillity of a forest clearing, or the vitality of a great city?

**C** I would recommend the seaside to sun-worshippers; and perhaps the countryside to claustrophobics.

**B** And yet I must reject two of them, as you are forcing me to make a choice.

**D** Cities are vibrant places, full of people working, relaxing, being tourists, rushing about, even just sitting and watching each other.

**E** I think of these holidays as more like a force 10 gale in the rush to be first to that precious little piece of fought-over sand.

# Varying your sentences

You will gain more marks if you use a range of different sentence structures. This means:

☑ mixing short, medium and long sentences

☑ including statements, questions, commands (direct address, using 'you') and exclamations

☑ including subordinate clauses, e.g. 'so that …', 'until …', 'in order to …', 'since…'

Note that deliberately repeating a word or sentence structure can also be effective, e.g. 'If you are affected, then I am affected.'

> **14 (a)** Read student 1's answer below. Explain why the examiner gave it an A grade for its use of sentence structure.
>
> **(b)** Then rewrite student 2's answer to boost its grade from grade D to C or above. Read the examiner's comment to help you.

## Student 1

> *Of course sport is good for us, they say. It's ridiculous to even contemplate that sport has a negative side: it's healthy, it makes us competitive and it gives us something to look forward to. How could you think otherwise? Well, many people do think otherwise, because sport can also harm.*

## Student 2

> *I love sport myself. I play for the school team at football. I watched the World Cup on TV. I also play cricket for a local club. I am very fit, I'm sure that is mainly because of all the sport I play, lots of people think you can get fit just by walking, that simply isn't true.*

**Sentence structure**

This student hasn't thought carefully enough about using a range of sentence structures. All the sentences are statements. The first few are all very short, and all begin with 'I': the repetition is not effective here. The second half of the paragraph is a string of statements separated by commas.

*Remember* to pay attention to punctuation. Punctuation makes the meaning of your sentences clear, and guides the reader through the text. In particular:

- **vary your punctuation** for effect. Don't just string statements together with commas: use colons, semicolons or begin a new sentence instead.
  'She's always smoked, smoking is disgusting' ✗
  'She's always smoked; smoking is disgusting.' ✓

- **remember the apostrophe** of possession (e.g. singer's) and omission (e.g. won't). NB it's = it is.

## A TO A*

Punctuation, grammar and spelling will have to be almost perfect if you want to get an A*. However, don't use an easy or dull word in order not to misspell a more interesting word – you will be given credit for showing a wide vocabulary.

You are now going to pull together all the learning you have done in this section by attempting a complete writing task. You will then study two other students' answers for comparison.

**15 a)** Answer the exam question below. You have 40 minutes.

**b)** Read the students' answers and examiner comments below. Complete the activities in the boxes.

> A newspaper is running a competition to win a holiday by the sea, in the country or in a city. To enter the competition, you must write a letter to the newspaper, stating which holiday you would choose and commenting on the reasons for your choice.

### Student 1

This student has thought about the form of the response – a letter. Where else can you see that this is the right form?

There is some attempt to vary sentence length here, but the long second sentence gets out of control. Rewrite it to make the sentence structure more effective.

This student could add a bit of 'sparkle' to the writing, e.g. by ending the paragraph 'In the meantime, I wouldn't choose Bournemouth or Barcelona.' Add or rewrite a sentence in the next paragraph to liven up the style.

The student has generally given a personal viewpoint, as this is what the question demands. In this paragraph, however, the viewpoint slips a bit. Identify where this happens, and rewrite to make the viewpoint consistent.

The student adopts a consistent tone – formal but with touches of humour. This is appropriate to the question. However, the tone becomes too informal at times in this paragraph – identify where, and rewrite.

1  Dear Editor,

Firstly, I would not put holidays by the sea at the top of my list. Holidays by the sea seem to be of two main types: either the very traditional British 'seaside town' holiday, which seem to be very old-fashioned, and therefore they do not appeal 5 much to my age group; or 'package-tour' holidays to overcrowded beaches in Spain, where you fight over your little bit of beach, or to put your towel down on a recliner first, and this does not appeal to me either, maybe if you could arrange for me to have a beach to myself, but with a range of modern facilities nearby, I might change my mind.

10  Next, I will consider holidays in the country. The countryside is supposed to offer peace and quiet, with lovely scenery. But some people prefer to be active on their holidays, with something interesting to do, so the peace and quiet will not suit them. Also, people who enjoy the sight of beautiful scenery usually find that coach loads of other people also enjoy the same sights, and at the same time. 15 As an example, my family went on a trip to Stonehenge last year, and we spent more time in a queue to get in and out of the car park than we did looking at the stones (and the photos I took of the stones all have about twenty complete strangers in them, as it was so crowded). As you can tell, I consider holidays in the country to be over-rated, and I would not choose one for myself.

20  Finally, then, I come to city holidays which we see advertised nowadays as 'City Breaks', this seems an odd name for them, as most people live in cities already... However, this kind of holiday would certainly be my choice. Cities are lively, busy places, and always have something to offer, for all age groups. You can go to museums, cinemas, theatres, sports or music events, shops, famous monuments 25 or attractions, or even just chill and enjoy the 'buzz' of people and activity. Every famous city has its attraction, and usually a 'downtown' area where people get together, just to have a look at each other if nothing else crops up. Paris has the Eiffel Tower, Amsterdam has its canals, New York has the Empire state Building, etc etc. Like you can enjoy a city holiday, even in your own city. Lots of Londoners, 30 for example, have never been on the London Eye, or a boat cruise down the River Thames, and these world-famous attractions are on their very own doorstep!

*City holidays can also be taken at any time, whereas holidays by the sea or in the countryside depend on the weather, for example, or on when families can go away in school holiday times. For me, there's no choice.*

*I hope that you (and your readers, if you publish my letter) can see clearly why I have chosen the city holiday over the other two.*

35 *Yours faithfully,*

> There is some attempt to end the letter well, but it is a bit dull. How could you make the ending more impressive?

## The examiner's view

Apart from the missing introduction, the organisation of the response is sound and straightforward: three alternatives are offered, with reasons given for each. The letter format is handled appropriately, and the chosen tone and style generally suit the task. Sentence structure shows some control and ambition (colons, etc.) but occasionally lets the student down. The enthusiasm of the response gives it quite a strong personal voice, though the voice and tone slip occasionally. The range of vocabulary is adequate, though not ambitious.

### A grade C

> **16** Assess your own answer against this C grade answer. Look at the 'Steps to success in writing' on page 9 to check how well you are meeting the assessment objectives. What do you need to work on to improve your grade?

### Student 2

1 *Dear Editor,*

*What a choice! How can I reject the waves crashing on the beach, or the tranquility of a forest clearing, or the vitality of a great city? And yet I must reject two of them, as you are forcing me to make a choice – and I*
5 *will try to reach my decision rationally and calmly.*

*Seaside holidays are the holidays of idyllic childhoods: rock pools, sandcastles, ice creams: even if you didn't have holidays like these yourself, that's how the seaside is portrayed in numerous television programmes and films. This image, though, is always somewhat old-fashioned, or even*
10 *nostalgic – the cars driving along the front are Morris Minors not Nissan Micras. Today, perhaps, the 'seaside holiday', as most people now think of it, is set in Spain, or on a Greek island. No doubt there will be lots of factor 20 in evidence – but I think of these holidays as more like a force 10 gale in the rush to be first to that precious little piece of fought-over sand.*
15 *Seaside holidays are not for me, then, I'm afraid: I don't hanker for the past, and I don't relish the seasonal stampede.*

*The calm and tranquil atmosphere of a holiday in the countryside should – we are told – contrast sharply with my vision of overcrowded beaches. But is this the reality of a rural retreat? No one can deny the charms*
20 *of rolling hills and valleys, and we can be in awe of the great mountain ranges or other natural phenomena – but we need to be able to appreciate them in the right conditions. If a particular 'beauty spot' is appealing to you, or to me, then it is certain to appeal to countless thousands of*

> How effective is the first paragraph as an opening? Does it (a) get the reader's attention, (b) set the right tone, and (c) introduce all sides of the issue? Compare this opening with Student 1's.

> The student uses a variety of punctuation to make the sentences longer and more interesting. Find two examples and say why they are effective.

> What tricks and techniques does the student use in this paragraph to liven up the style? Check back to the list on page 152 above.

others... and a high percentage of them always seem to get there just before me. Of course it is possible to immerse oneself in 'the country' away from particular attractions: but then other aspects of country life tend to creep in to our consciousness, those aspects that are rather less well publicised in the brochures. In ascending order of size, I have in mind anything from midges to cockerels which wake you up in the morning, to farm dogs which chase you when you're cycling, to tractors which block you on the 'quaint' country lanes, to the cement quarry which suddenly dominates your view. As you can see, I speak from experience: the famous 'peace and quiet' of the countryside seems like a myth, to me.

We always seem to link 'myth' with 'reality', and for me 'reality' is the essence of what cities offer. Cities are vibrant places, full of people working, relaxing, being tourists, rushing about, even just sitting and watching each other. For me, this is the point of a city, and it is at the heart of why I would make a city holiday my choice. The comment could be made that cities are crowded, noisy, restless places which harbour criminals – but in a way that's their whole point (well, not the criminals, obviously). I feel drawn to the 'life' which every big city seems to generate, as though I am revitalised just by being part of the great whirl of humanity. Of course the famous cities have their famous attractions – there's only one Eiffel Tower or Empire State Building – but these only serve as a focal point for all the human activity which takes place around them. It goes without saying that there is always plenty to do in a big city, with the concentration of museums, galleries, shops, and so on... but in a sense that isn't the point for me, as I don't particularly want to 'do', I prefer just to 'be'.

I hope, then, that I have given my comments to you (and, I hope, to your reader) in a way which leaves no doubt about my choice. I would recommend the seaside to sun-worshippers; and perhaps the countryside to claustrophobics; but for me a City Centre is the centre of the world.

Yours faithfully,

Note that this student also takes the straightforward planning route of commenting on one holiday choice in each paragraph. The paragraphs are also linked cleverly, e.g. the use of 'myth' here links with the end of the previous paragraph. How are the other paragraphs linked to give a well-crafted response?

How does this ending sum up the question and the student's answer effectively?

## The examiner's view

This is a very polished piece of writing. The task is carried out in a sharply focused and consistent way, and the tone and style are appropriate to this light-hearted topic of holidays. The vocabulary is wide, and is used with precision and imagination. Although the structure is quite straightforward, the paragraphs are linked in a subtle way. A range of punctuation and grammatical devices is used with assured control.

**A grade A\***

**17** Assess your own answer against this A\* grade answer. Look at the 'Steps to success in writing' on page 9 to check how well you are meeting the assessment objectives. What do you need to work on to improve your grade?

## 5 Exam question practice

Now is the time to put everything in this section into practice for yourself.

**18** Allow 40 minutes, and choose one of the questions below.

When you have finished, assess yourself against your answer to the question in Activity 15, or swap your work with your partner and assess each other's. Look back at the 'Steps to success in writing' on page 9 to identify where you are doing well and where you need to improve. Note down three areas in which you would like to improve, and practise those skills.

*Remember* that you cannot practise too much. Areas such as planning, writing good openings and signposting your answer will improve very quickly when you practise.

**1** Think of an occasion when you felt like an outsider.

Write about this, analysing your thoughts and feelings at the time.

*(Higher Tier)*

**2** 'Makeovers' of rooms or personal image are popular subjects for both magazine articles and TV programmes.

Comment on the reasons why you would change, or not change, **either** your image **or** your room.

*(Higher Tier)*

**3** A website magazine wants video contributions from teenagers on the topic of 'image' with reference to personal appearance, including hairstyle and fashion.

Write the text for a talk commenting on this subject, to be delivered directly to camera.

The magazine wants you to give your views as fully as possible and provide answers to the following questions:

❖ how easy and important is it to be yourself?
❖ how much are teenagers influenced by the media and celebrities like pop stars and models?
❖ how much influence do parents and teachers have?
❖ what image would you like to present of yourself?

*(Foundation Tier)*

**4** Write about a meal which was memorable.

Review the whole meal, giving the reasons why it was so memorable.

You could write about any features which made it special, such as:

❖ the setting
❖ the occasion
❖ the food
❖ the service.

*(Foundation Tier)*

### EXAM TIP

- Spend no more than a few minutes thinking about and planning your answer.
- Begin with an introduction and sum up with a thoughtful conclusion.
- Make sure your tone, voice, form and content (TV FC) match the purpose and audience of the task.
- Vary your sentence structure and punctuation, and signpost your sentences.

# Glossary

**Adjective:** a word that describes or gives extra detail about a noun, making the writing richer and more interesting. E.g. 'they would be scrutinized from behind the **murky** windscreen by Miss Shepherd' (*The Lady in the Van*, p. 55). The use of the adjective 'murky' helps the reader build up a picture of the scene. Sometimes there is more than one adjective. E.g. In *Vendetta* (p. 89), the widow and her son live in a '**small, mean** house' (p. 89).

**Adverb:** a word that describes a verb or gives extra detail about how the action of the verb is carried out. Like adjectives, adverbs make the writing richer and more interesting. E.g. 'the bride and the groom stood **respectfully** to one side while the wedding party crowded into the new ger' (*Mongolian Wedding*, p. 46). The adverb 'respectfully' helps to make the contrast between the verbs 'stood' and 'crowded' more effective. In *Digging* (p. 21), the bottle is 'corked **sloppily** with paper'. The adverb 'sloppily' tells the reader *how* the bottle is corked.

**Alliteration:** repetition of the initial consonant sound of words for effect, commonly used in poetry:
'Rats lived in the foundations,
**s**ending **s**couts under the **s**tairs' (*The House*, p. 6)
The effect of alliteration is often to emphasise and draw attention. Here the repeated s sound emphasises the rhythm of the line, and also maybe suggests the faint sound of rats scuttling under floorboards.

**Anecdote:** a true story from personal experience. Anecdotes are a useful technique for supporting points you are making in your writing. E.g. 'Mobile phones have made arrangements so much easier. For example, my neighbour was going to pick us up from the concert but his car broke down. He was able to phone us…'

**Assonance:** The repetition of a vowel sound for effect.
'An ecstasy of **fumbling**,
Fitting the **clumsy** helmets just in time' (*Dulce et Decorum Est*, p. 13)
The two words in bold are linked by assonance, and this stresses the soldiers' panicky rush to fit the gas helmets.

**Atmosphere:** the overall mood of a piece of writing, evoking a certain feeling or emotion in the reader. E.g. the atmosphere of *The House* (p. 6) could be described as chilling, grim and unwelcoming.

**Audience:** the intended reader for a piece of writing, or listeners to a speech. Awareness of audience affects the way you write: you would write very differently for an adult audience than you would for an audience of your peers.

**Cliché:** a phrase which has been used too often, and so loses its impact, e.g. 'The summer holidays are **in full swing**' ('Mind games', p. 62). 'In full swing' helps to paint a familiar picture.

**Colloquial:** usually the language of informal conversations; not the sort of language you would normally use in formal settings, such as in letters to people you do not know. Writers will sometimes adopt a colloquial, conversational style of writing to suit their purpose and audience, and to give their writing a humorous tone. E.g. 'My experience of physical education in school consisted of running up muddy hills… as the technical teacher had a fag.' ('Sport in Schools', p. 63)
(See also *formal/informal writing*)

**Emotive language:** language which produces an emotional response. E.g. 'mobs of teenage gangs' is emotive because it suggests something threatening; 'groups of young people' is more neutral language.

**Evaluation:** a judgement about whether or not something is successful or effective. The student answer on p. 127 of this book discussing an article by George Alagiah contains evaluation: 'Words such as 'quiet… lonely' evoke pathos and allow his readers not only to empathise with him, but to picture the dying. This brings the emotion and pain to his writing which makes it so compelling.'

**Fact:** true information; real events. Facts can be checked and shown to be true, e.g. 'Due to a piece of legislation called the Title IX, passed in 1972, girls are guaranteed equal spending and support in school sport.' ('School sports culture leads to violence', p. 61)
(See also *opinion*)

**Formal/informal writing:** in some situations, such as applying for a job, or writing to someone you have not met, formal writing is appropriate. This means avoiding slang or colloquial expressions, and keeping to the accepted rules of correctness regarding grammar and vocabulary. At other times, a more informal tone is appropriate, such as writing a letter to a friend. Writers use a range of tones for different purposes: a warm, informal tone as in 'Sport in schools' (p. 63), where the writer is expressing a personal viewpoint; a more formal tone in 'Parents learn how to say NO' (p. 64), where the writer is reporting other people's views. Note. Never be *too* informal: text message language is not acceptable in your examination answers!

**Form of writing:** a type of writing with its own conventions of layout and style. The most common types of writing you might be asked to write for GCSE English are letter, speech, article, leaflet and report.

**Imagery:** the use of language to create images or pictures in the reader's mind, usually by comparing one thing with another. *Similes* and *metaphors* are two examples of imagery.

**Metaphor:** a way of describing something by comparing it with something else, e.g. 'The darkness **crumbles** away' (*Break of day in the trenches*, p. 46). The darkness cannot literally 'crumble'; the word vividly expresses how the darkness gradually fades.

**Noun:** a word for a person (Henry), a place (London), a thing (the desk) or a quality or idea (courage; poverty).

**Objective** (opposite: *subjective*): if you are objective in your writing, you are basing your points on facts and not on your feelings. Analytical writing, in which you might be asked to consider advantages and disadvantages in a balanced answer, calls for objective writing. E.g. 'It is difficult to be objective about your own children.' Cherry Norton, the writer of 'Pay your children too much attention' (p. 65) is reporting other people's views rather than expressing her own, and is therefore writing objectively.

**Onomatopoeia:** the use of a word which sounds like the action it describes. The iguana 'came **rustling** across my path' (*Iguana Memory*, p. 38). 'The **squelch** and **slap**/ Of **soggy** peat' (*Digging*, p. 21). The sound of 'rustling' suggests the dry, dusty sound of the iguana moving; in 'squelch', 'slap' and 'soggy' you can hear the sound of the wet peat being dug and stacked. Note how the *alliteration* of the letter s adds to the effect.

**Opinion**: a personal point of view or belief; not a fact which can be checked. Other people may well disagree with an opinion. E.g. 'Chris King, 15, thinks smacking is acceptable sometimes' ('Smacking not the answer, say kids', p. 66).

**Organisation and paragraphs:** prose writing is usually structured into paragraphs, separating and ordering the main points, with a new paragraph for each new topic or idea. This makes the ideas and the overall argument much easier for the reader to follow, and can also create effects for the reader. E.g. compare the detailed and comprehensive research in 'Mind games' (p. 62) with the one-line paragraphs offering the writer's opinion in 'Sport in Schools' (p. 63).

**Presentational features**: the way material is visually presented to the reader, also called the layout. This is particularly important in media texts, where the overall impact is created by a combination of words and visual features. Presentational features include use of pictures, colour, variety of font, overall design, tables and charts.

**Rhetorical techniques or devices**: ways of trying to persuade your audience to your point of view or to a course of action. Techniques include:
* **repetition**: 'The health benefits are clear. The social benefits are clear.' ('Sport in schools', p. 63)
* **contrast**: opposing points of view or ideas set against each other, as in this example: 'The mother or father who slaps needs help, they do not need to be turned into criminals' ('Use persuasion not coercion', p. 65)
* **exaggeration:** 'swimming past the icebergs in the Battery Park' ('Sport in schools', p. 63)
* **lists**: 'Those not in the 'in-group' become the subjects of bullying, taunting and ridicule. They are the nerds, dweebs etc.' ('School sports culture leads to violence', p. 61). Lists often consist of three items. Audiences seem to respond to the rhythm of a list of three, and they are therefore common in speeches. Winston Churchill said to the nation as World War II began: 'I have nothing to offer but blood, toil, tears and sweat', but the speech soon became famous as the 'blood, sweat and tears' speech. People clearly believed it sounded better as a list of three!
* **rhetorical question**: a question which does not require an answer, but which makes a point by apparently inviting the reader to give an opinion. E.g. 'Even the best of good parents sometimes snap – should that be made a crime?' ('Use persuasion not coercion', p. 65)

**Setting**: the time (historical period, year, time of day) and the location of a story. Linked to these aspects may be specific cultural or social conditions that are important to the story. E.g. *Country Lovers* is set on a South African farm during the Apartheid era, and this forms the backdrop to the events of the story.

**Signpost words and phrases**: words and phrases which guide the reader through the piece of writing by connecting one idea to another, also called connectives. Some are particularly useful in analytical or argumentative writing, where you might be weighing up opposing points of view (e.g. however; on the other hand; although; whereas; in contrast; alternatively). Others help you to summarise your ideas at the end of an argument piece (e.g. in

conclusion; therefore; generally). Some are useful when writing to inform or explain to show cause and effect (e.g. because; consequently, as a result).

**Simile**: like a metaphor, a simile describes something by comparing it with something else, the difference being that it uses the word 'like' or 'as…as'. It is important to identify the qualities being compared when commenting on the effect of a simile. 'His shoulders globed like a full sail' (*Follower*, p. 20) is a visual simile appealing to the sense of sight. The trout 'slips like butter down/the throat of the river' is a simile referring to the sense of touch (*Trout*, p. 45).

**Subjective**: (opposite: *objective*) subjective writing is influenced by personal opinions. It does not attempt to be balanced; it presents a personal viewpoint. E.g. 'He is too subjective to be a good critic.' The writer of 'Use persuasion not coercion' (p. 65) is expressing personal views and therefore writing subjectively.

**Tone**: also known as the mood, tone is the writer's attitude towards the topic. E.g. the tone might be serious, light-hearted, angry, sarcastic, sad. The tone of *Warning* (p. 29) is defiant; the tone of *Dulce et Decorum Est* is both sad and angry; *Mongolian Wedding* has a humorous tone.

**Verb**: a word or group of words which describes an action, experience or state. A verb is always in a particular *tense*, past, present or future.
* **Past**: 'She **died** in the upstairs bedroom' (*Death in Leamington*, p. 8)
* **Present**: 'Through the window I **see** no star' (*The Thought-Fox*, p. 36)
* **Future**: 'I **shall spend** my money on brandy' (*Warning*, p. 29)

**Viewpoint**: the point of view or perspective from which the story is told. The identity of the writer can affect how the reader sees the characters and events of the story or how the reader reacts to the topic being discussed. E.g. in 'Use persuasion not coercion' (p. 65) the viewpoint is that of a parent who has experience of the 'intensity and relentlessness' of parenting, whereas in 'Smacking not the answer, say kids' (p. 66), the viewpoints are those of young people: 'Memories of being hit by a parent can stand out more than any other single event for many teenagers like Paul.'

**Voice**: the narrator or person speaking in a text. The voice could be:
* **first person**: the narrator refers to himself or herself by using I or we, as in *Warning* (p. 29). Note that the narrator 'I' is often the writer pretending to be someone else.
* **second person**: the narrator uses 'you' as in *You will be hearing from us shortly* (p. 7). This is not very common.
* **third person**: the narrator uses 'he', 'she', 'it', 'they' or a name, as in *Death in Leamington* (p. 8).

Page numbers in the Glossary refer to the Edexcel Anthology unless otherwise indicated.

Published by:
Edexcel Limited
One90 High Holborn
London
WC1V 7BH
www.edexcel.org.uk
© Edexcel Limited 2007

Distributed by:
Pearson Education Limited
Edinburgh Gate
Harlow
Essex
CM20 2JE
www.longman.co.uk

First published 2007
Second impression 2008
ISBN: 978-1-84690-168-3

Edited and typeset by Ken Vail Graphic Design
Cover and text design by Ken Vail Graphic Design
Cover image courtesy of Alamy Images
Printed and bound in China  SWTC/02

Acknowledgements
The authors and publisher are very grateful to Mandy Hill for her expert contribution to this book. The publisher is grateful to Julia Strong for use of the concept of PEC.

We are grateful to the following for permission to reproduce copyright material:
p93 'Keep Warm Keep Well' leaflet produced for the Department of Health, reprinted with permission; p94 'Bombs Hurt Kids' text from First News, page 3, 15–21 Sept 2006, reprinted with kind permission; p95 'The useful thing would be teaching them how to read' by Edward Enfield, The Daily Mirror, Friday, December 27 2002, reprinted with permission of Solo Syndications; photograph of Edward Enfield © BBC, reprinted with permission; p97 'Riding Skills' © Crown Copyright, reprinted with permission; p101 'Shreddy Plant At My Hamster' by Andy Russell, The Sun, Saturday June 3rd 2006, reprinted with permission of NI Syndications, photograph © Liverpool Echo, reprinted with permission; p102 'The Great Hamster Escape (starring Mike)' found in The Guardian, 3 June 2003, text © Liverpool Echo, photo © Liverpool Echo, diagram © The Guardian, all reprinted with permission; pp106-107 'Your Guide to Beach Safety' Beach Lifeguards, reprinted with permission; p112 First Light by Geoffrey Wellum, (Penguin Books 2002) © Geoffrey Wellum 2002 reprinted with permission of Penguin Books UK; p112 Silvertown: An East End Family Memoir by Melanie McGrath, published by 4th Estate © Melanie McGrath 2002, reprinted with permission of HarperCollins Publishers UK; p113 Hokkaido Highway Blues: Hitchhiking Japan by Will Ferguson, first published in Great Britain by Canongate Books Ltd, 14 High Street, Edinburgh EH1 1TE, © Will Ferguson, reprinted with permission of Canongate Books; p113 'Compromise is King' by Diana Appleyard from www. thistravel.co.uk © Diana Appleyard, reprinted with the kind permission of the author; p113 The Beaver Book Of Horror by Daniel Farson, Hamlyn 1979; p116 'Compromise is King' by Diana Appleyard from www.thistravel.co.uk. © Diana Appleyard, reprinted with the kind permission of the author; p117 Further Travellers Tales From Heaven And Hell edited by Dan Hiscocks, published by Eye Books, reprinted with permission; p118 First Light by Geoffrey Wellum, (Penguin Books 2002) © Geoffrey Wellum 2002 reprinted with permission of Penguin Books UK; p120 Silvertown: An East End Family Memoir by Melanie McGrath, published by 4th Estate © Melanie McGrath 2002, reprinted with permission of HarperCollins Publishers UK; p123 reproduced with permission from London, ed. 4 © 2004 Lonely Planet Publications; p125 A Passage To Africa by George Alagiah published by Little Brown, 2001, reprinted with permission.
Photos: p11 iStockphoto; p14 photos.com; p15 iStockphoto; p17 www.ww1photos.com; p22 photos. com; p26 photos.com; p34 stockxchng/Roberttheu; p40 iStockphoto; p50 photos.com; p53 Ogilvy; p58 iStockphoto; p67 photos.com; p74 iStockphoto; p82 iStockphoto; p85 stockxchng/fearthecat; p94 photos. com, stockxchng/ozdv8;  p95 © BBC; p97 Stockxchng/2sogar, Stockxchng/bSpear, Stockxchng/bSpear, photos.com; p101/102 © Liverpool Echo; p113 photos.com; p118 Stockxchng/TueRomanow; p119 Stockxchng/Leonbidon; p131 photos.com; p132 photos.com; p134 photos.com; p137 photos.com; p138 photos.com; p149 photos.com; p152 photos.com.
Every effort has been made to trace the copyright holders and we apologise in advance for any unintentional omissions. We would be pleased to insert the appropriate acknowledgement in any subsequent edition of this publication.